Prompting Python for Full Stack Development

Learn Python Programming by Building Full-Stack Web Apps, Automation Projects, Data Tools, and AI Applications

Temidayo Adefioye

www.orangeava.com

First Published: April 2026

Published By: Orange Education Pvt Ltd, AVA®

Address: 9, Daryaganj, Delhi, 110002, India

275 New North Road Islington Suite 1314 London,
N1 7AA, United Kingdom

ISBN (PBK): 978-93-49887-08-4

ISBN (E-BOOK): 978-93-49887-61-9

Scan the QR code to explore our entire catalogue

www.orangeava.com

Get a Free eBook

We hope you're enjoying your recent book purchase! Your feedback is incredibly valuable to us and helps other readers discover books that truly make a difference.

If you found this book useful or enjoyable, we'd greatly appreciate it if you could leave a short review with a 5-star rating on Amazon. Your review supports our work and allows us to reach more learners worldwide.

As a thank-you, we're happy to offer you a **free digital copy of this book** plus a **30% discount code** for your next purchase on our official websites:

www.orangeava.com

www.orangeava.in (For the Indian Subcontinent).

☑ **How it works:**

Leave your review on Amazon, take a screenshot of the confirmation or use the following link to submit the claim and email it to **info@orangeava.com.** Once received the required detail, we will send your rewards within 24 hours, **along with one month free subcription to the book on AVA SkillShelf!**

Claim Form
https://rebrand.ly/4d2477

Thank you for your support—it truly means a lot to us.

Enjoy 1 Month of Free Access to AVA SkillShelf!

The future belongs to lifelong learners. With AVA SkillShelf, you go beyond reading books and start building real, job-ready skills curated by industry experts.

Your membership unlocks **200+ learning products** covering AI, Cloud, Python, Cybersecurity, Data Science, DevOps, and more—all in one platform. Our bestselling technical books are transformed into structured courses designed for practical, real-world application.

Learn directly from experienced professionals and published authors, with no filler—just actionable insights. Earn **verified digital certifications** to strengthen your CV, LinkedIn profile, and professional credibility.

Learn anytime, anywhere, on any device, at your own pace. Ideal for students, professionals, career switchers, and tech leaders.

For full access to all current and future courses, choose our **Annual Membership**. Simply scan the QR to get started!

For 1 month Free access, simply refer to the steps on the previous page titled: Get a Free ebook!

https://www.avaskillshelf.com/

Downloading the code bundles and colored images

Please follow the links or scan the QR codes to download the
Code Bundles and Images of the book:

https://github.com/ava-orange-education/Prompting-Python-for-Full-Stack-Development

The code bundles and images of the book are also hosted on
https://rebrand.ly/d7d3a7

In case there's an update to the code, it will be updated on the existing GitHub repository.

Errata

We take immense pride in our work at **Orange Education Pvt Ltd,** and follow the best practices to ensure the accuracy of our content to provide an indulging reading experience to our subscribers. Our readers are our mirrors, and we use their inputs to reflect and improve upon human errors, if any, that may have occurred during the publishing processes involved. To let us maintain the quality and help us reach out to any readers who might be having difficulties due to any unforeseen errors, please write to us at:

errata@orangeava.com

Your support, suggestions, and feedback are highly appreciated.

Dedicated to

My Beloved Parents:
Adefioye Clement Olusegun,
Adefioye Esther Olubanke.
And
My Beautiful Wife, Olaronke Adefioye.

About the Author

Temidayo Adefioye is a software developer, talent leader, and social impact advocate with over a decade of experience at the intersection of technology, education, and workforce development. His work is driven by a simple mission: expanding access to opportunity and equipping professionals with the skills needed to thrive in a global workforce.

An accomplished author, Temidayo has published five internationally recognized books in the last three years, distributing thousands of free copies to underserved communities as part of his commitment to democratizing knowledge. As a LinkedIn Learning instructor, his courses have reached over 30,000 learners worldwide, offering practical guidance on technical skills, career growth, and professional development.

He is the founder of Talenvo, a platform addressing Africa's work-experience gap by connecting emerging talents to meaningful work opportunities, and helping companies build reliable and competent teams. Through this work, he has developed innovative products that improve hiring, workplace experience, and career readiness.

Beyond technology, Temidayo leads Switchcon, a non-profit supporting university students through mentorship, career events, and internship bootcamps, with many participants securing interviews and employment. He also hosts the annual Workfront Summit, bringing together global speakers and thousands of participants to explore the future of work.

Temidayo's vision is bold and clear, that is to reduce unemployment in Africa, and prepare a new generation of globally competitive talents.

About the Technical Reviewer

Rahul Kumar Thatikonda is an Analytics Architect and Voting Member of the Python Software Foundation, dedicated to professionalizing the practice of Data Science. A recognized industry professional with over a decade of experience and a Master of Science in Business Analytics, he specializes in architecting decision intelligence frameworks and digital transformation strategies for highly regulated sectors, including healthcare, life sciences and financial services.

As an active researcher in Legacy Modernization, Rahul focuses on solving a critical global challenge: upgrading complex industrial infrastructure without the risk of total system replacement. His independent work on "Agentic AI" and resilience frameworks has demonstrated the ability to increase order processing throughput by over 117%, and reduce billing compliance errors by 75%.

Dedicated to advancing the competitive edge of the global AI landscape, Rahul codifies the engineering rigor necessary for large-scale industrial resilience. By advocating for high-performance, "Production-First" architectures, he provides a standardized roadmap for modernizing the international workforce and mission-critical supply chain infrastructure. His work bridges the gap between theoretical AI and safe industrial application, ensuring that data science delivers transformative value which is not only accurate but defensible, compliant, and engineered to support complex interests on a global stage.

Acknowledgments

I am deeply grateful to God for His wisdom and guidance throughout this journey. His presence has been my constant source of insight and clarity, giving me the strength and direction to write this book. Without His guidance, nothing would have been possible.

I thank my parents for believing in me from the very beginning of my career in 2010. Their support, encouragement, and faith in my potential have carried me through every challenge and milestone, and I dedicate a part of this work to them.

I thank my beautiful wife for always encouraging me to push further. We got married as I was about to start this book in 2025, and her love and belief in me made the journey lighter, and more joyful.

A special shout out to the editorial team at Orange Education Pvt. Ltd., my publisher, for their patience, guidance, and overall support in bringing this book to life.

Preface

The world of software development is evolving faster than ever, and Artificial Intelligence (AI) is at the center of this transformation. AI is no longer a futuristic concept; it is a practical tool that can enhance the way we write, review, and deliver code. This book is written to guide developers on how to harness AI as a collaborator.

Throughout this book, we explore how AI can simplify complex programming tasks, from understanding Python code to building interactive applications, and automating repetitive workflows. You will learn to use AI to explain algorithms, identify inefficiencies, generate optimized codes, and even build projects such as basic games, data reports, and AI-powered web applications. Each chapter is designed to give hands-on, practical experience, helping you to move confidently from concept to implementation.

Chapter 1: This covers getting started with AI-assisted development. It explains why AI is a career advantage today, and guides readers through setting up Python, Jupyter Notebook, VS Code, and integrating ChatGPT into their workflow. Readers will generate their first Python script with AI, and learn how to approach coding with a collaborator mindset.

Chapter 2: It focuses on understanding Python code with AI. Here, AI acts as a mentor to explain syntax, logic, and algorithms in simple English. The chapter also demonstrates how to improve readability, enforce the best practices, and refactor messy scripts into clean, professional-grade programs.

Chapter 3: It introduces problem decomposition and prompt engineering. Readers will learn how to break down complex problems into manageable steps, and craft precise prompts for AI. Practical examples guide learners in moving from vague requests to functional Python solutions in data analysis, automation, and web tasks.

Chapter 4: This explores debugging and refactoring with AI. Readers will learn how to identify errors, trace bugs, and apply AI-suggested fixes. The chapter also demonstrates refactoring techniques to make the code cleaner, modular, and easier to maintain.

Chapter 5: This chapter teaches automating tedious tasks. Readers will use Python automation libraries with AI to script repetitive tasks like file management, web scraping, and report generation, creating reusable solutions that save time and reduce errors.

Chapter 6: This shows how to make an interactive game. Using Python and AI, readers will design and implement a simple game, covering logic, user input, and visuals, while learning how AI can brainstorm mechanics, generate functions, and assist in debugging gameplay.

Chapter 7: It introduces Natural Language Processing (NLP) through an authorship identification program. Readers will analyze text, extract features, and build models to detect writing patterns, gaining practical NLP experience, and using AI-guided Python workflows.

Chapter 8: This focuses on automating data reports. Readers will learn how to process, analyze, visualize, and report data automatically with Python and AI, creating professional-quality outputs, while eliminating repetitive work.

Chapter 9: It guides readers in building an AI-powered web application. From backend scaffolding with Flask or FastAPI to frontend integration and real-time AI features, learners will create a functional web app with hands-on guidance throughout.

Chapter 10: This chapter covers the best practices and optimization. Readers will learn to write clean, efficient, and maintainable codes, leveraging AI for refactoring, performance improvements, documentation and collaboration, preparing them for professional-grade Python development.

DID YOU KNOW

Did you know that Orange Education Pvt Ltd offers eBook versions of every book published, with PDF and ePub files available? You can upgrade to the eBook version at **www.orangeava.com** and as a print book customer, you are entitled to a discount on the eBook copy. Get in touch with us at: **info@orangeava.com** for more details.

At **www.orangeava.com**, you can also read a collection of free technical articles, sign up for a range of free newsletters, and receive exclusive discounts and offers on Print Books and eBooks.

PIRACY

If you come across any illegal copies of our works in any form on the internet, we would be grateful if you would provide us with the location address or website name. Please contact us at **info@orangeava.com** with a link to the material.

ARE YOU INTERESTED IN AUTHORING WITH US?

If there is a topic that you have expertise in, and you are interested in either writing or contributing to a book, please write to us at **business@orangeava.com**. We are on a journey to help developers and tech professionals to gain insights on the present technological advancements and innovations happening across the globe and build a community that believes Knowledge is best acquired by sharing and learning with others. Please reach out to us to learn what our audience demands and how you can be part of this educational reform. We also welcome ideas from tech experts and help them build learning and development content for their domains.

REVIEWS

Please leave a review. Once you have read and used this book, why not leave a review on the site that you purchased it from? Potential readers can then see and use your unbiased opinion to make purchase decisions. We at Orange Education would love to know what you think about our products, and our authors can learn from your feedback. Thank you!

For more information about Orange Education, please visit **www.orangeava.com**.

Table of Contents

CHAPTER 1
Getting Started with AI-Powered Development

Introduction

Every major shift in technology starts with a mindset change, from how we write software to how we imagine what is possible. The rise of AI-assisted coding is one of those moments. It is not just a productivity hack; it is a transformation in how developers think, create, and collaborate.

This chapter introduces you to the exciting world of AI-assisted development, where human intuition meets machine intelligence. You will learn why AI is changing how developers code, the tools that make it possible (such as ChatGPT and GitHub Copilot), and how to set up your workspace to get the most out of them. Most importantly, you will begin to see that coding with AI is not about replacement; it is about amplification.

By the end of this chapter, you have gone from hearing about AI in tech headlines to actually generating your first Python script with it. That is your first milestone, and the beginning of a new kind of partnership between human creativity and machine precision.

Structure

In this chapter, we will cover the following topics:

- The Rise of AI-Assisted Coding: Why it is a career advantage today:
    - From Manual Coding to AI Collaboration
    - How AI Changes the Developer's Role
    - The Smart Developer's Advantage
- Overview of ChatGPT, GitHub Copilot, and AI Developer Assistants:
    - AI Developer Assistants

    - GitHub Copilot: The Pair Programmer for Every Line
    - ChatGPT: Your AI Mentor in a Console
    - Other AI Assistants: The Ecosystem Expands
- Setting up Python (3.11+) and VS Code for an AI-friendly Workflow:
    - Step 1: Installing Python
    - Step 2: Installing VS Code: The Developer's Home Base
    - Step 3: Optimizing Your Workspace for AI Development
    - Step 4: Setting up Virtual Environments (Your Personal Sandbox)
    - Step 5: Installing Core Libraries
- Integrating ChatGPT into Development: Web UI or Extension:
    - Option 1: ChatGPT Desktop Application (Web UI)
    - Option 2: ChatGPT Browser Extension / IDE Integration
    - When to Use Each
- Practical Walkthrough: Generating Your First Python Script with AI:
    - Step 1: Pick a Simple, Real-World Problem
    - Step 2: Understand the Prompt-Response Flow
    - Step 3: Review, Learn, and Do Not Just Copy
    - Step 4: Experiment and Extend
    - Step 5: Run It Locally
    - Step 6: Think Like a Developer
- The Mindset Shift: Coding with a Collaborator, not a Crutch:

The Rise of AI-Assisted Coding: Why It is a Career Advantage Today

There is a quiet revolution happening in the world of software development, one that is rewriting not just codes but the very definition of what it means to be a developer.

A few years ago, "AI in coding" sounded like a Silicon Valley fantasy! Today, it is your daily reality. Developers are brainstorming with ChatGPT, debugging with GitHub Copilot, documenting with Cody, and even designing system architectures through conversational prompts. Hence, whether you realize it or not, the keyboard is no longer your only tool -- your AI collaborator has joined the team.

From Manual Coding to AI Collaboration

Think back to when autocomplete first entered IDEs; it felt magical. Now imagine that magic, multiplied by a thousand. AI-assisted development takes context from your codebase, documentation, and even the bugs you have fixed before to predict your next move. It does not just complete your line, it suggests *why* and *how* to write it better.

Instead of starting from a blank screen, developers today start from a conversation. You describe the problem, the AI scaffolds the logic, and you refine it with your unique judgment, a workflow that saves hours of boilerplate, and endless Stack Overflow searches.

But is AI Not Coming for Developers?

That is the question echoing across every developer forum and tech event: If AI can code, do we still need coders?

AI may write code faster, but it cannot understand why the code matters. It does not feel user frustration, business urgency, or the creative thrill of solving an impossible problem. What AI is replacing is not developers, it is developer drudgery.

The debugging loops. The syntax errors. The repetitive code reviews. By offloading these, AI lets developers focus on what cannot be automated: thinking, designing, and innovating.

In essence, AI-assisted coding does not make you less valuable, it makes you irreplaceable. Because when everyone can code, the advantage shifts to those who can think critically, and communicate with machines effectively.

How AI Changes the Developer's Role

AI is not just a productivity hack; it is a career multiplier. Those who learn to leverage it early gain a superpower: the ability to go from idea to prototype at record speed.

Here is how the role of a modern developer is evolving:

- **From Typist to Architect:** You are no longer defined by how much code you write, but how intelligently you direct the AI to generate and refine it.
- **From Debugger to Decision-Maker:** With AI handling low-level errors, developers can focus on system design, scalability, and product vision.
- **From Executor to Educator:** Great developers will teach AI, training it with better prompts, examples, and context. The future of coding is as much about *coaching your AI teammate*, as it is about coding yourself.

The Smart Developer's Advantage

While some developers fear AI will take their jobs, the most forward-thinking ones are already landing better ones because of it.

Employers now value developers who can collaborate effectively with AI tools, not compete against them. Knowing how to prompt ChatGPT, validate outputs, and optimize AI workflows has become a core skill in modern software engineering interviews.

AI-assisted coding is not the end of programming; it is the evolution of it. The ones who thrive will be those who adapt, experiment, and learn to code with the rhythm of AI, not against it.

So yes, AI is rewriting the rules of development.

The real winners are not machines.

They are the humans who learn to speak with machines fluently.

Overview of ChatGPT, GitHub Copilot, and AI Developer Assistants

There was a time when writing codes felt like solving puzzles in the dark, with hours of trial and error, endless tabs open, and Stack Overflow posts bookmarked like treasures. Then came a drastic revolution: AI developer assistants. They did not replace our keyboards; they simply changed how we thought while typing.

At first, these tools felt like superpowers. You would start typing a line in VS Code, and suddenly a full function appeared, correctly formatted and often more efficient than your first attempt. It was not long before engineers began to notice a subtle shift: they were spending less time searching documentation for syntax, and more time designing better logic.

The developer's workflow was evolving rapidly.

AI Developer Assistants

Think of them as your always-awake coding partner who never complains, always remembers the docs, and has a near-infinite memory of the world's codebases. AI assistants analyze what you are writing, predict what you are trying to do, and offer smart suggestions that can save minutes, sometimes hours of development time.

They do not just autocomplete your thoughts; they interpret intent. When you write,

```
# calculate average temperature from a list of readings.
```

They know you are about to need a loop, a sum, and a length check, and they will propose it instantly.

But let us break down the players leading this movement.

GitHub Copilot: The Pair Programmer for Every Line

GitHub Copilot was one of the first tools to make developers genuinely rethink productivity. Built on OpenAI's Codex model, it integrates directly into editors such as VS Code and JetBrains, offering real-time code suggestions as you type.

Copilot learns from billions of lines of open-source code. It recognizes context, function names, docstrings, and even your projects structure as well as predicts the next logical block. It is like having a senior engineer telling you, "Here is what I would write next."

Its greatest strength lies in seamless integration. You do not have to switch tools or prompt it in chat. It just works inside your IDE, adapting to your rhythm.

However, its limitation is also its strength; Copilot focuses mainly on writing. It is brilliant for quick scaffolding, but does not explain why a certain code block was chosen or how you could improve it. It is like copying a good answer, without understanding that the reasoning is useful, but at the surface-level.

ChatGPT: Your AI Mentor in a Console

This is the conversational side of coding. While Copilot writes, ChatGPT teaches. It is not bound by your editor; it can explain recursion, help you think through algorithmic trade-offs, or debug an error line by line, all through natural conversation.

You can ask ChatGPT things like:

> "*Why does my Flask app hang when I restart the server?*"

And it would not just fix it; it will unpack the "why". It can show you alternate implementations, refactor your logic for clarity, and even explain what is happening under the hood in plain English.

For this reason, this book leans heavily on ChatGPT. You will learn not just *how to prompt it* for working codes, but also how to use it as a thinking partner to reason, question, and challenge your own solutions.

AI-assisted coding is not about typing faster. It is about understanding deeper.

Other AI Assistants: The Ecosystem Expands

While Copilot and ChatGPT dominate headlines, they are not alone. Amazon CodeWhisperer, Tabnine, and Replit Ghostwriter all aim to blend AI with development workflows in slightly different ways:

- **Amazon CodeWhisperer** integrates closely with AWS services, generating cloud-ready code that fits AWS best practices.
- **Tabnine** focuses on local code learning. It trains on your private repositories to suggest completions that match *your code style.*
- **Replit Ghostwriter** is popular among students and solo developers, making full-stack web apps easier by completing both front-end and back-end snippets directly in the browser.

Together, these tools represent a **new era of development** where speed meets understanding, and coding becomes more about problem-solving than memorizing syntax.

Most developers treat ChatGPT like a shortcut generator: paste a question, grab a solution, and move on. But we will take a different path.

In this book, ChatGPT is your learning lab. You will learn:

- How to craft prompts that produce clear, maintainable codes.
- How to debug collaboratively, understanding error messages, instead of just patching them.
- How to refactor smarter, optimizing readability and performance with AI feedback.
- How to build full projects, where ChatGPT acts as a technical consultant, not just an assistant.

Each chapter will show not only *what ChatGPT outputs*, but *why it works*, *how to interpret*, *critique*, *and improve* that code like a professional.

AI can write the code, but only you can understand the problem.

And that is where mastery begins.

Setting up Python and VS Code for an AI-Friendly Workflow

You cannot build a modern house without quality tools, and the same goes for coding with AI. Before we start building intelligent scripts and projects, we need a setup that feels *like home*, fast, reliable, and ready to talk to ChatGPT when you are.

This section walks you through preparing your environment and installing **Python (latest stable release)** and **Visual Studio Code (VS Code)**, the two core tools that will carry you throughout this book. But beyond installation, we will also fine-tune your workspace to be **AI-friendly**, meaning you will write, test, and iterate codes seamlessly, while collaborating with ChatGPT.

Step 1: Installing Python

Python is the heartbeat of everything you will do in this book. Its simplicity, versatility, and massive ecosystem make it the most AI-compatible programming language today.

However, this is important, versions change fast. AI frameworks such as OpenAI's ChatGPT, LangChain, or FastAPI evolve constantly. So, do not fix your environment to an outdated version number just because you saw it in a tutorial. Always check the official Python website for the latest stable release (at the time of reading this, it might be Python 3.14.0 or newer).

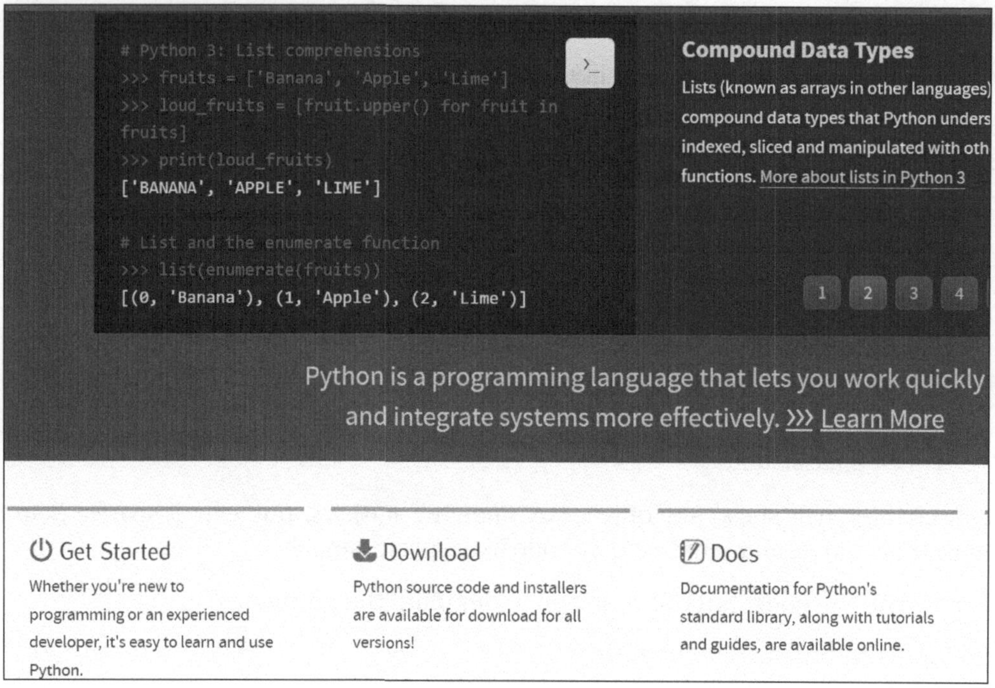

Figure 1.1: *Python Official Website*

Installation Checklist:

1. Go to python.org/downloads.
2. Download the latest version for your operating system (Windows, MacOS, or Linux).

3. During installation, check the box that says "**`Add Python to PATH`**" — this single checkbox saves countless headaches later.

   Verify your installation by opening your terminal and typing:

   ```
   python -version
   ```

4. If you see something like Python 3.12.x, you are good to go.

   That is your engine installed; now let us set up the code editor.

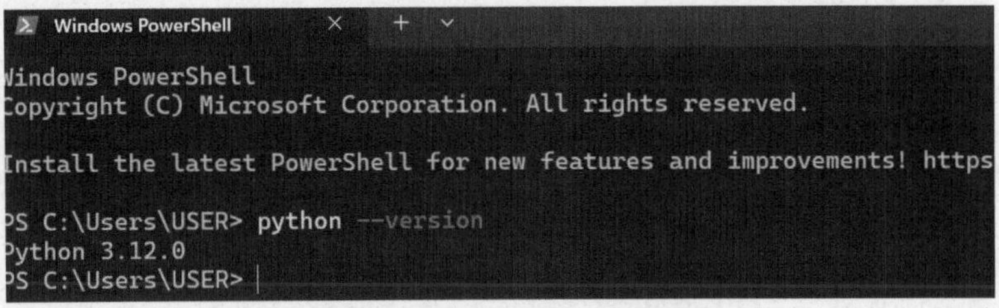

Figure 1.2: *Python Version*

Step 2: Installing VS Code: The Developer's Home Base

Visual Studio Code (VS Code) is more than just a text editor; it is a developer's homebase designed for speed, clarity, and intelligent integration. It is lightweight, open-source, and the go-to IDE for millions of developers using AI tools like GitHub Copilot or ChatGPT plugins.

Installation Steps:

1. Head to code.visualstudio.com.
2. Download the latest stable build for your operating system.
3. Follow the installation wizard.
4. Launch VS Code, and you should see a clean interface with a side panel, editor space, and terminal option.

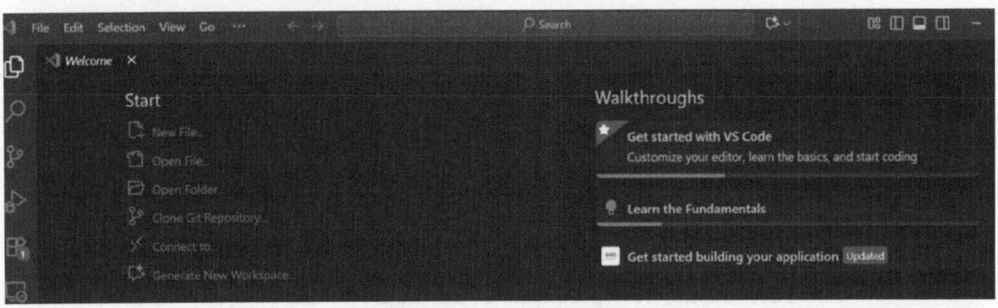

Figure 1.3: VS Code Editor

Quick Setup Tips for Beginners:

Go to **`View → Terminal`** to open an integrated terminal. You will run your Python Code right inside VS Code – no switching windows.

- Under **`Extensions`**, install "Python" by Microsoft (this adds syntax highlighting, debugging, and linting).
- Optionally, install **`Pylance`** for intelligent type checking, and autocompletion.

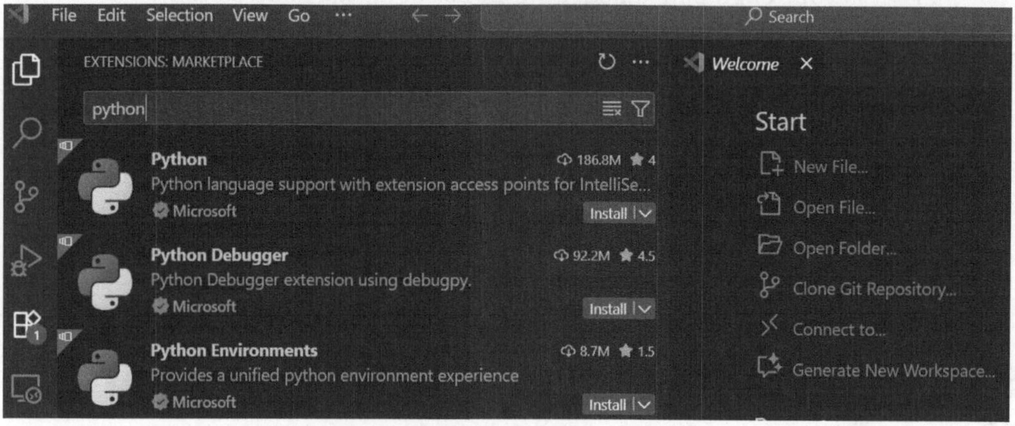

Figure 1.4: VS Code Editor Extensions

Step 3: Optimizing Your Workspace for AI Development

Now that both Python and VS Code are ready, let us make them AI-*smart*.

AI development thrives on **context**, so your environment should feel like a collaboration space — not just a text editor. Here is how to prepare for that:

Must-Have VS Code Extensions

- **GitHub Copilot (Optional but powerful)**
  - Integrates AI code suggestions directly into your editor.
  - Shortcut: *Ctrl + Enter* (Windows) *or Cmd + Enter* (Mac) to trigger suggestions.
- **ChatGPT Extension (by OpenAI or third-party)**
  - Let us now chat directly with ChatGPT from within VS Code. We will set this up in the next section.
  - You can highlight a piece of code, right-click, and ask "Explain this" or "Refactor this."

    - Perfect for real-time learning as you code.
- **Python Docstring Generator**
    - Helps you generate structured docstrings with one click, a good habit for writing clean, AI-readable code.
- **Auto Rename Tag / Bracket Pair Colorizer**
    - Keeps your syntax visually clean. You will appreciate this when debugging nested functions or HTML templates.

Step 4: Setting up Virtual Environments (Your Personal Sandbox)

One common mistake beginners make is installing **every Python library globally** on their computer. This often leads to version conflicts, one project breaks another, dependencies stop working, and debugging becomes frustrating.

To avoid this, you will create a virtual environment (`venv`) for each project.

A virtual environment is a self-contained Python installation that belongs to only one project. It has:

- Its own Python interpreter.
- Its own installed libraries.
- No impact on other projects on your system.

Thus, you can think of it as your projects private lab, isolated, controlled, and reproducible.

Creating a Virtual Environment

Open your project folder in VS Code, then open the terminal inside VS Code (`View → Terminal`).

Run the following command:

```
python -m venv
```

This creates a new folder called `venv` inside your project. This folder contains everything Python needs to run this project independently.

Activating the Virtual Environment

After creating the virtual environment, you must activate it. Activation tells your system and VS Code which Python environment to use.

On Windows:

```
venv\Scripts\activate
```

On macOS/Linux:

```
source venv/bin/activate
```

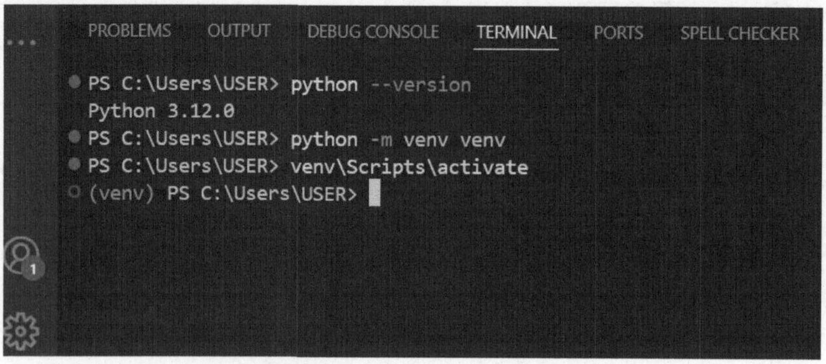

***Figure 1.5**: Python Virtual Env Setup*

When activation is successful, you will see (**venv**) at the beginning of your terminal prompt. This is your confirmation that the virtual environment is active.

What Activation Means inside VS Code

When a virtual environment is activated:

- VS Code automatically detects, and uses the Python interpreter inside the venv folder.
- Any libraries you install using **`pip`** go only into this projects environment.
- When you run Python files, VS Code executes them using this isolated environment, not your system-wide Python.

In other words:

> VS Code now "locks" your project to this virtual environment.

This prevents accidental global installs, and ensures that your project behaves the same on any machine.

Installing Libraries

With the virtual environment activated, you can now install libraries such as:

```
pip install requests
```

That library is installed only for this project. Other projects remain unaffected.

Step 5: Installing Core Libraries

Once your environment is ready, let us prepare the essentials you will use across projects in this book:

```
pip install request  s pandas matplotlib
```

- **Requests**: for making API calls.
- **Pandas**: for data manipulation and analysis.
- **Matplotlib**: for visualizing trends and reports later.

You can always add new libraries as needed per chapter. The goal here is to ensure that your baseline toolkit is ready for AI collaboration.

By now, your system should have:

- The latest version of Python installed and working.
- VS Code customized with relevant extensions.
- A clean virtual environment for isolated development.
- Core libraries installed for data and API work.

You have officially built your *playground*. From this point onward, every project, every script, and every experiment will live here with ChatGPT as your constant companion.

Perfect — here is how we can write **Subsection 3: Integrating ChatGPT into Development** (two pages worth of engaging, educative, and practical content). It covers both the **desktop version** and **extension**, compares them clearly, and adds **insider developer tips** and **warnings** that make it feel like a senior engineer is mentoring the learner.

Integrating ChatGPT into Development

Let us get practical. You have seen what ChatGPT can do; now let us bring it into your actual workflow.

When it comes to integrating ChatGPT into your daily development environment, there are two main approaches:

1. **Using the Desktop Application (Web UI)**
2. **Using a Browser Extension inside your IDE or code editor**

Both have their place. The goal here is to show you how to set them up, when to use each, and how to avoid common mistakes developers make when integrating AI into their workflow.

Option 1: ChatGPT Desktop Application (Web UI)

The desktop (or web) version is the **official ChatGPT interface** provided by OpenAI. You can access it via your browser at chat.openai.com or through the desktop app (available for Windows and macOS).

It gives you full access to the ChatGPT interface with features like:

- Chat history
- File uploads
- Image understanding
- Code generation with syntax highlighting
- Project-specific memory (depending on your plan)

Installation (Desktop/Web)

1. Visit **https://chat.openai.com**.
2. Log in or sign up.
3. Optionally, download the **desktop app** from the same page (you will find the link under your profile menu).
4. Once installed, you can pin it to your taskbar or **dock** for quick access, and like a coding assistant living beside your IDE.

How Developers Use It

Here is how many developers integrate it into their day-to-day:

- **Code Debugging:** Paste your error trace, describe the bug, and ask for possible causes.
- **Learning APIs Quickly:** Drop documentation snippets and ask, "Summarize this for me and give usage examples."
- **Generating Unit Tests:** Feed it a function and ask, "Write Jest tests for this."
- **Refactoring:** Paste an old code block, and ask for a cleaner version.

Pros

- No setup needed — works out of the box.
- Access to all GPT capabilities (including code, vision, and file analysis).
- Supports file uploads (for example, log files and code snippets).
- Generous free plan with many uses daily.

Cons

- No direct IDE integration (you switch between browser/app and code editor).
- Can be slower, if your internet is poor.
- Requires manual copy-paste between environments.

Keep a pinned chat called **"Code Assistant"** in your ChatGPT sidebar. Use it as your dedicated workspace; that way, your debugging, refactoring, and architecture discussions all live in one thread, and the model builds context over time.

Option 2: ChatGPT Browser Extension / IDE Integration

This is where things get exciting. Extensions bring ChatGPT *inside your code editor* (like VS Code, JetBrains IDEs, or even Chrome DevTools). They connect through your **OpenAI API key**, meaning the extension talks directly to the model behind the scenes.

Installation Steps (Example: VS Code Extension)

1. Open **`VS Code:`** Go to the **`Extensions`** tab (*Ctrl* + *Shift* + X).
2. Search for "**`ChatGPT`**" or "**`CodeGPT`**."
3. Choose a trusted extension (for example, *CodeGPT by Daniel San* or *ChatGPT: Copilot for* VSCode).
4. Install the extension.
5. When prompted, paste your **OpenAI API key** (you can get one from your OpenAI dashboard under platform.openai.com).

Treat your API key like a password.

Before proceeding, read these rules carefully:

- Never share your API key with anyone.
- Never commit your API key to GitHub or any public repository.
- Never paste your API key into code files, screenshots, or blog posts.
- Use the extensions secure settings field only.
- Regenerate your key immediately, if you believe it has been exposed.

You can generate or revoke API keys from your OpenAI dashboard at:

`platform.openai.com`

How Developers Use It

Once connected, you can:

- Highlight a piece of code → Right-click → "`Explain with ChatGPT`."
- Generate docstrings, comments, or tests inline.
- Get autocomplete suggestions as you type (in some plugins).
- Interact directly in a side panel, similar to pair programming with an AI.

Pros

- Seamless integration — no need to switch tabs.
- Great for quick questions or code explanation while working.
- Speeds up code review and documentation writing.
- Highly customizable (depends on the extension).

Cons

- Requires your API key — usage is deducted from your OpenAI balance.
- API tokens can run out quickly with frequent use.
- Some extensions are unofficial — privacy risk if they log your code.
- Missing some advanced web features (such as file uploads or GPT-4V).

If you are on a budget, use the extension only for **on-the-spot tasks** (for example, explain, summarize, or refactor a snippet).

Then, switch to the desktop version for heavy-lifting conversations like debugging, architecture planning, or dataset analysis — where the context window is larger, and free usage is more generous.

When to Use Each

Think of it like this:

- **Desktop/Web = Strategy Mode:** Long conversations, full projects, teaching moments.
- **Extension = Execution Mode:** Quick help while coding, doc generation, or syntax hints.

Using both strategically gives you a hybrid workflow that feels like having an AI co-pilot who lives in your IDE but also joins you for design meetings.

Thus, whether you prefer to chat in a browser tab or use commands in your IDE, you are now equipped to bring AI directly into your workflow.

Practical Walkthrough: Generating Your First Python Script with AI

At this point, you have set up ChatGPT.

You have seen how to integrate it into your developer workflow. Now it is time to roll up your sleeves, and build your first real script, powered by AI.

Let us make this your first *aha moment*, where you realize AI is not replacing developers; it is supercharging them to be more efficient.

Step 1: Pick a Simple, Real-World Problem

Before writing any code, start with *intent*. What do you want the script to do?

Instead of a random "Hello, World", we will make something a little more useful. Let us say we want to automate renaming files in a folder, a simple, practical task that saves minutes daily.

So, we will tell ChatGPT:

"*Write a Python script that renames all files in a folder, replacing spaces with underscores.*"

That is it. You have just written your first AI prompt as a developer.

Step 2: Understand the Prompt-Response Flow

When you hit "*Enter*", ChatGPT will respond with something like this:

```
from pathlib import Path

folder_path = Path("test_folder")
for file in folder_path.iterdir():
    if file.is_file() and " " in file.name:
        new_name = file.name.replace(" ", "_")
        file.rename(file.with_name(new_name))
print("Files renamed successfully!")
```

Let us break it down:

- `Path("test_folder")`

  Refers to a folder named **`test_folder`** inside your project directory. This is called a relative path, and it works the same on Windows, macOS, and Linux.

- `folder_path.iterdir()`
  Loops through every item inside that folder.
- `file.is_file()`
  Ensures that the script only renames files (not subfolders).
- `" " in file.name`
  Checks whether the filename contains a space.
- `file.rename(file.with_name(new_name))`
  Renames the file by replacing spaces with underscores.

Before running this script:

1. Create a folder named **`test_folder`**
2. Place it inside your project directory
3. Add a few files with spaces in their names

Now pause and breathe. You did not Google it. You did not scroll Stack Overflow. You simply described what you needed in plain English and got working code.

That is the first superpower of integrating AI into your coding life: You spend more time thinking, less time searching.

Step 3: Review and Learn, Do Not Just Copy

Many learners make a classic mistake here; they copy, paste, and move on. Do not. This is your moment to learn from the AI.

Ask ChatGPT follow-up questions like:

> *"Can you explain what `os.listdir` does?" "How can I make sure it only renames `.txt` files?" "What if the folder does not exist?"*

Each time you ask, you deepen your understanding, the AI acts like a mentor, and not a search engine.

Step 4: Experiment and Extend

Now, let us go one level deeper.

You can tell ChatGPT:

> *"Modify the script so that it logs all renamed files into a `rename_log.txt` file."*

It will likely respond with something like:

```
from pathlib import Path
# Folder inside your project directory
```

```
folder_path = Path("test_folder")

# Log file will be created in the project root
log_file = Path("rename_log.txt")

with log_file.open("w") as log:
    for file in folder_path.iterdir():
        if file.is_file() and " " in file.name:
            new_name = file.name.replace(" ", "_")
            new_file = file.with_name(new_name)
            file.rename(new_file)
            log.write(f"{file.name} → {new_name}\n")

print("Files renamed and logged successfully!")
```

Before running the script:

1. Make sure your project folder is open in VS Code
2. Inside that project folder, create a new folder called **`test_folder`**
3. Add a few files with spaces in their names (for example: **`my file.txt`**)

The script will:

- Rename the files inside **`test_folder`**
- Create **`rename_log.txt`** in the same directory as your Python script

Why `pathlib` is a better choice:

- Using **`pathlib`** gives you several advantages:
- Paths are treated as objects, not strings
- No need to manually join paths (**`os.path.join`**)
- Code is cleaner and more readable
- Works consistently across operating systems

For example:

```
file.name          # filename
file.is_file()   # check if it's a file
file.rename()     # rename the file
```

And there it is, a more complete, more useful tool, in seconds. You can tweak it, personalize it, or even package it for others to use.

This task just described what "AI-assisted coding" means in practice: you describe the goal, and then refine through dialogue.

Step 5: Run It Locally

If you are on your computer:

a. Open **VS Code** or any code editor.

b. Copy the script and save it as **`rename_files.py`**.

c. Create a test folder with some sample files.

d. Run in terminal:

```
python rename_files.py
```

You will instantly see your files renamed, and a log file created.

Congratulations, you just built your first working Python automation, co-authored with ChatGPT!

Step 6: Think Like a Developer

Do not stop at "it works". Ask the kind of questions experienced engineers ask:

- What happens if two files have the same new name?
- Can we make this cross-platform (Windows + macOS)?
- How do we turn this into a command-line tool?

Ask ChatGPT those follow-up questions.

That is how you move from an AI *user*: AI *developer.*

The Mindset Shift — Coding with a Collaborator, Not a Crutch

Let us get one thing clear: AI is not here to make you lazy. It is here to make you efficient.

When people first start using ChatGPT or Copilot, they often fall into two camps:

1. **The Dependents**: Those who use AI to do all the thinking for them.
2. **The Collaborators**: Those who treat AI as a partner that amplifies their reasoning.

Only one of these groups thrives in the long run.

Coding with AI is not about speed; it is about *precision of thought.* The better you can describe a problem, the more accurate, and elegant your AI-generated code becomes.

Your value as a developer will increasingly lie in your clarity of problem definition, not just your syntax recall.

AI can write code. But it cannot truly understand your products context, goals, or users.

That is still your territory.

Think of ChatGPT as your pair programmer, a colleague who never sleeps, does not judge, and occasionally surprises you with a cleaner solution.

The danger of AI is not that it replaces coders; it is that it tempts them to stop thinking like one. If you copy and run code without asking why it works, you stop learning. If you question, experiment, and rework what AI gives you, you evolve faster than ever.

So, whenever ChatGPT hands you a solution, pause and ask:

> "*What if I did it another way?*"
>
> "*What is the trade-off of this approach?*"
>
> "*How would a human engineer refactor this?*"

Those questions keep your brain in the driver seat, exactly where it belongs.

The future belongs to developers who can speak both human and machine. You will describe intent in natural language, co-create solutions with AI, and fine-tune code.

So, as you continue through this book, remember this simple rule:

> "*Do not let AI think for you; let it think with you.*"

This is because the moment you make that shift, coding stops feeling like labor... and starts feeling like creation again.

Conclusion

AI-assisted development is happening already. The developers who thrive in this new landscape are not the ones who resist change but the ones who learn how to use it with curiosity, balance, and purpose. You now understand how to set up an AI-powered workflow, how ChatGPT fits into your development environment, and most importantly, how to treat it as a collaborator.

In *Chapter 2*, you will learn where AI fits into the development workflow, what it does well, and where human judgment is still essential. The next chapters will take you deeper into practical skills: understanding code using AI, decomposing problems, automating tasks, and even building intelligent systems.

For now, take a moment to celebrate; you have just stepped into one of the most important skill shifts of this decade.

Points to Remember

- AI-assisted coding is not about replacing developers but augmenting their creativity and efficiency.
- ChatGPT, GitHub Copilot, and other AI tools can help you code faster, debug smarter, and learn quicker, but you remain the decision-maker.
- Always install the latest versions of Python and VS Code for better compatibility and performance.
- Using the ChatGPT desktop version offers more generous usage than the extension that depends on API keys.
- Treat AI as a pair programmer, not a one-click solution.
- The true skill is not in writing code fast; it is in understanding and communicating problems clearly.
- Always ask "*why*" behind the code AI generates. That is how you grow.
- Think of coding as a conversation, you and AI co-creating something useful, beautiful, and efficient.

Assessment

Let us test your understanding of this chapter. Try answering this short exercise before checking the solution.

Use ChatGPT to generate a simple Python script that prints "*Hello, AI World!*" and modifies the message using a variable (for example, **`user_name = "Sam"`**). Then, ask ChatGPT to refactor the code to make it more flexible (for example, using a function).

Solution

```
# Step 1: Basic Script
user_name = "Sam"
print(f"Hello, AI World! Welcome, {user_name}.")

# Step 2: Refactored Script using AI's suggestion
def greet_user(name):
    return f"Hello, AI World! Welcome, {name}."
print(greet_user("Sam"))
```

CHAPTER 2
Understanding Python Code with AI

Introduction

In recent years, Artificial Intelligence (AI) has transformed the way we learn, write, and understand code. Python, being one of the most popular programming languages, is widely used across industries from web development to data science. However, for beginners and even intermediate programmers, understanding existing Python code can sometimes be challenging due to complex logic, unfamiliar libraries, or large codebases.

This chapter explores how AI can assist in understanding Python code. We will discuss tools, techniques, and practical approaches that leverage AI to interpret code, generate explanations, and even suggest improvements. By the end of this chapter, you will have a clearer picture of how AI can become a coding companion, making Python code more accessible, easier to debug, and faster to learn.

Structure

In this chapter, we will cover the following topics:

- Using AI to Explain Python Syntax, Logic, and Algorithms in Plain English
  - Why This Matters More Than You Think
  - Explaining an Algorithm
  - Be Curious and Iterative
- Leveraging AI to Understand Third-Party Libraries and Unfamiliar Codebases
  - How AI Turns Confusion into Clarity
  - Reading a Data Pipeline You Did Not Write
  - Building Intuition around Libraries

- Learning from Projects instead of Tutorials
- Use ChatGPT such as a Code Reviewer and Not a Wikipedia Page

- AI-Assisted Walkthroughs of Complex Data Structures (for example, Nested Lists, Dictionaries, and Classes)
    - How AI Makes Complex Data Structures Less Intimidating
    - Turning AI into Your Personal Data Navigator
    - Using AI to Debug Confusing Data
    - Exploring Classes and Objects through Conversation
    - Real-World Learning Practice
    - The Secret Advantage
- Improving Code Readability with AI (Comments, Docstrings, and Naming Conventions)
    - Using AI to Generate Meaningful Comments
    - Crafting Docstrings
    - Naming Conventions
    - Real-World Example
    - Consistency over Cleverness
    - Building a Readable Mindset
- AI as a Tool for Enforcing Python Best Practices (PEP 8 Compliance, Modularity)
    - Using AI to Ensure PEP 8 Compliance
    - Encouraging Modularity
    - Structuring Larger Projects
    - Detecting Anti-Patterns
    - Building a Habit of Best Practices
- Using AI to Summarize and Refactor Legacy
    - Summarizing Messy Codebases
    - Refactoring Step by Step
    - Identifying Redundant or Dead Code
    - Rewriting Legacy Functions Efficiently
    - Building Confidence with Gradual Refactoring
    - Legacy Project Rescue

- Hands-on Exercises: Feeding Real-World Open-Source Snippets into AI for Explanation and Optimization
    - Selecting Open-Source Snippets
    - Asking for an Explanation
    - Optimizing the Snippet
    - Experimenting with Multiple Snippets
    - Lessons from Real-World Code
    - Building a Practice Routine

Using AI to Explain Python Syntax, Logic, and Algorithms in Plain English

If you have ever stared at a piece of Python code and wondered, "Okay... but what *exactly* is happening here?", you are not alone. Every developer, whether beginner or advanced, has that moment when code looks more like a puzzle than a solution.

That is where AI, especially **ChatGPT**, becomes your personal interpreter.

Think of it this way: you already *speak* logic, you simply need someone to translate the syntax for you. ChatGPT does exactly that. It translates loops, conditions, and algorithms into meaningful stories you can actually relate to.

Let us say you are working with this code snippet:

```
for i in range(5):
    print(i * 2)
```

If you ask ChatGPT:

> *"Explain this code like I am a 10-year-old."*

It might respond with something like:

> *"This code tells the computer to count from 0 to 4. For each number, it multiplies it by 2 and shows the result."*

Quite simple, right? That is the power of natural-language understanding—it bridges the gap between what the computer reads and what your brain interprets.

Why This Matters More Than You Think

Understanding code is not just about memorizing syntax; it is about reading intent. When you use AI to break down code, you train yourself to think like a computer and an instructor. That is a rare combination and an invaluable career skill.

Here is what you can do with ChatGPT while learning something new:

1. **Clarify Unfamiliar Syntax**

   Ask: "*Explain what the* ***args** *and* ****kwargs** *mean in a Python function.*" ChatGPT will not just define it — It will show examples, analogies, and even compare them to real-life scenarios ("like packing multiple gifts into one box").

2. **Understand Logic Flow**

   You can paste an entire function and ask, "Describe step-by-step what happens when this function runs."

3. **Deconstruct Algorithms**

   You want to understand recursion, search algorithms, or sorting logic? AI can walk you through them visually, describing what happens in memory, and iteration by iteration.

4. **Ask for Analogies**

   Sometimes, technical explanations do not stick, but analogies do. For example, ChatGPT can explain recursion like:

   "*Imagine standing between two mirrors. Each mirror reflects the other endlessly — that is what recursion feels like.*"

Explaining an Algorithm

To understand how AI explains logic, let us start with a classic example: The Bubble Sort algorithm.

```
def bubble_sort(arr):
    n = len(arr)
    for i in range(n):
        for j in range(0, n - i - 1):
            if arr[j] > arr[j + 1]:
                arr[j], arr[j + 1] = arr[j + 1], arr[j]
    return arr
```

Bubble Sort is often used in education because its behavior is easy to follow. It repeatedly compares neighboring values and swaps them if they are out of order, like gently shaking a container until everything settles into place.

If you paste this into ChatGPT and ask:

> "*Explain this in simple English.*"

You will likely receive a clear explanation that walks through the logic step by step.

You can even go further:

> "*Explain this visually.*"

ChatGPT may produce a step-by-step illustration of how values move through the list—an instant clarity boost for many learners.

While Bubble Sort is useful for learning, it is not efficient for real-world applications.

- Time complexity: `O(n²)`
- Performance degrades quickly as data grows.
- Rarely (if ever) used in production systems.

This distinction is critical:

Readable code is not always good code. Educational algorithms are not always practical.

Python already provides highly optimized sorting algorithms built into the language.

```
numbers = [5, 3, 8, 1, 2]
sorted_numbers = sorted(numbers)
```

Or, if you want to sort in place:

```
numbers.sort()
```

These use Timsort, a hybrid algorithm designed for real-world data. It is:

- Fast,
- Stable,
- Optimized in C, and
- Trusted in production systems.

Instead of accepting the first algorithm you see, try asking:

> "*This algorithm works, but it seems inefficient. Can you suggest a more efficient approach using Python best practices?*"

Or:

> "*Compare Bubble Sort with Python's built-in sorting.*
>
> *When should each be used?*"

This teaches you how to:

- Evaluate AI-generated code,
- Recognize performance trade-offs, and
- Ask better follow-up questions.

Be Curious and Iterative

When you are using AI to understand Python, do not just stop at one explanation. Ask *follow-up questions*, that is, where the secret source is.

- *"Show me the same algorithm but using a `while` loop instead."*
- *"How does this code's time complexity compare to selection sort?"*
- *"Can you simplify this logic using Python's built-in functions?"*

Each time, you are not just learning code; you are learning how to think about code.

Leveraging AI to Understand Third-Party Libraries and Unfamiliar Codebases

Reading your own code from last month can already feel like an unresolved crime scene. Now imagine jumping into a stranger's 10,000-line project with custom classes, weird variable names, and five different libraries you have never used.

That is not just intimidating; it is complete chaos in curly braces.

Before the introduction of Generative AI, you would spend hours switching between Stack Overflow tabs, official docs, and random GitHub gists. Today, that experience looks completely different. You can drop into a project, paste a chunk of code into ChatGPT, and ask:

> *"Walk me through what this function does and what library features it depends on."*

Within seconds, you will get a guided breakdown that reads like an annotated code review from a senior engineer who knows the codebase inside out.

Before sharing any company or project code with generative AI tools, always confirm with your manager or team lead first. These tools learn from the data you provide, which means any proprietary, sensitive code could unintentionally become exposed or influence public models. It is better to stay cautious than risk leaking intellectual property.

How AI Turns Confusion into Clarity

Every library from Pandas and NumPy to FastAPI and Requests has its own logic, conventions, and peculiar behaviors. Instead of manually decoding how it all fits together, AI can act as a real-time interpreter that helps you learn how to think inside a new ecosystem.

Here is how you can use ChatGPT to shorten the "what on earth is going on here?" phase:

Summarize Unfamiliar Functions or Modules

Paste a code block or an import statement such as:

```
from fastapi import FastAPI, HTTPException
```

Then ask:

"*What does each imported component do, and how are they typically used together?*"

You will instantly get practical insight instead of generic documentation links.

Map Relationships inside a Codebase

You can ask AI to describe dependencies and flow:

"*Explain how these functions connect, what gets called first, and what is returned?*"

Decode Unfamiliar Error Messages

Suppose you run into something like:

```
AttributeError: 'DataFrame' object has no attribute 'append'
```

You can ask:

"*Why am I getting this error, and what is the alternative?*"

ChatGPT will remind you that **`append()`** was deprecated and replaced with **`pd.concat()`**, saving you from outdated tutorials.

Simplify Documentation into Examples

Instead of reading long documentation pages, you can paste in sections and say:

"*Summarize this doc in simple terms and give me a working example that does the same thing.*"

Suddenly, documentation becomes a practical example.

Reading a Data Pipeline You Did Not Write

Let us say you inherit a project that transforms CSV data into visual insights using Pandas and Matplotlib. Here is a sample snippet:

```
data = pd.read_csv("sales.csv")
data["total"] = data["price"] * data["quantity"]
grouped = data.groupby("region")["total"].sum()
grouped.plot(kind="bar")
```

You could ask ChatGPT:

> "*Explain what this script does step-by-step, and describe what each library is contributing.*"

The response might sound like this:

> "*This script reads a CSV file called* `sales.csv`, *calculates total sales per record, groups them by region, sums up the totals, and then uses Matplotlib to visualize the results as a bar chart.*"

You can go further:

> "*Show me how to modify this to also include average sales per region.*"

This kind of learning feels active. You are literally playing detective with a copilot.

Building Intuition around Libraries

AI helps you develop intuition. Over time, you will start recognizing patterns in how libraries are structured:

- **Data Libraries** (such as Pandas, NumPy, Polars): Focused on transformation and vectorized operations.
- **Web Frameworks** (such as Flask, FastAPI, Django): Rely on decorators, routing, and request handling.
- **Automation Tools** (such as Selenium, PyAutoGUI): Interact with systems and UI components.

When you feed these into ChatGPT, it contextualizes them. It shows how they work, when to use them, and when to avoid them.

Learning from Projects instead of Tutorials

One of the smartest ways to grow as a developer is to study real-world repositories, but they can be overwhelming.

Let us say you have just cloned a GitHub repo. Before diving in, you can prompt ChatGPT:

> "*Summarize this project from the README and key files. What problem does it solve, and how is the architecture organized?*"

It can give you:

- A short project overview,
- Key folders and their purposes,
- Main dependencies, and

- The likely execution flow.

From there, you can ask it to trace specific functions, rewrite outdated code, or suggest where to start debugging.

Use ChatGPT Like a Code Reviewer

When you ask why something was written the way it was, ChatGPT becomes much more insightful. For instance:

> "*Why did the developer use a generator instead of a list here?*"
>
> "*What is the performance trade-off between this approach and using NumPy directly?*"

Those are the questions that teach you judgment, not just knowledge. Over time, your reasoning improves, and that is what separates good developers from pragmatic ones.

AI-Assisted Walkthroughs of Complex Data Structures

Data structures can sometimes be exhausting. You finally figure out how lists work, and then you meet *nested lists*. You understand dictionaries, then someone introduces *classes* and *objects*, and suddenly, you are staring at your screen.

How AI Makes Complex Data Structures Less Intimidating

When you encounter a deeply nested list or dictionary, the main struggle is not *how to access the value*, but *understanding what the structure even looks like*. That is where ChatGPT thrives.

You can copy your data structure and simply ask:

> "*Can you explain what this structure represents in plain English?*"

Here is an example:

```
data = {
    "students": [
        {"name": "Aisha", "scores": {"math": 88, "science": 92}},
        {"name": "David", "scores": {"math": 75, "science": 85}},
    ]
}
```

You might know this is a dictionary that contains a list, which contains dictionaries that contain another dictionary... but what does that mean practically?

You can ask ChatGPT to *unpack* it:

> "*Explain this data structure step by step as if I am new to Python.*"

And you will get a simple breakdown like:

- `Data` is a dictionary with one key: `"students"`.
- The value of `"students"` is a list containing two items.
- Each item is a dictionary that holds a `"name"` and a `"scores"` dictionary.
- The `"scores"` dictionary holds two subjects and their corresponding marks.

That is an explanation you can visualize and actually remember.

Turning AI into Your Personal Data Navigator

Here is where it gets more practical. Let us say you are trying to access David's science score. You could manually count your way through:

```
data["students"][1]["scores"]["science"]
```

But if you are still learning how indexing and keys work, that might feel confusing. Instead, you could ask:

> "*How can I access David's science score from this structure?*"

ChatGPT will walk you through not just the syntax but *why* it is written that way. It may even show multiple approaches, for example, using loops or list comprehensions, and explain when each is better.

That is what makes this powerful: you are not memorizing; you are *understanding through guided repetition.*

Using AI to Debug Confusing Data

It is easy to get lost when debugging large structures. Maybe, you are working with JSON data from an API, and you keep getting `KeyError` or `TypeError`.

Instead of staring at your screen, wondering why Python is messing with you, you can paste the problematic section into ChatGPT and ask:

> "*Why am I getting a KeyError when I try to access `user["address"]["city"]`?*"

It will often detect the missing key, show you how to verify with `print(data.keys())`, and even suggest defensive programming techniques such as:

```
user.get("address", {}).get("city", "Unknown")
```

This helps you develop the habit of writing safer and smarter code.

Exploring Classes and Objects through Conversation

When you move from lists and dictionaries to *classes*, Python suddenly starts feeling more abstract.

A class is basically a custom data structure, one that groups variables (attributes) and functions (methods) under one roof.

Here is a simple example:

```
class Student:
    def __init__(self, name, scores):
        self.name = name
        self.scores = scores

    def average(self):
        """
        Calculates the average score.
        Returns 0 if no scores are present.
        """
        if not self.scores:
            return 0
        return sum(self.scores.values()) / len(self.scores)
```

Now, you can ask ChatGPT:

> "*Can you explain what this class does, like I am a beginner?*"

It might say something like:

- A `Student` object represents one student.
- Each student has a `name` and a `scores` dictionary.
- The **`average()`** method calculates the average score.

Then, you could go deeper:

> "What happens when I call `student1.average()`?"

ChatGPT will explain that Python automatically passes the object (`student1`) into the method as `self`, and the function operates using the object's internal data.

This kind of back-and-forth builds genuine comprehension, not just surface familiarity.

Real-World Learning Practice

Let us do a small exercise.

Paste this snippet into your Python editor and try to explain what is happening. Then, ask ChatGPT to confirm or clarify your understanding.

```
library = {
    "fiction": [
        {"title": "1984", "author": "Orwell", "copies": 4},
        {"title": "Dune", "author": "Herbert", "copies": 2}
    ],
    "nonfiction": [
        {"title": "Sapiens", "author": "Harari", "copies": 3}
    ]
}

# Example task:
# Find all fiction titles with more than 2 copies
titles = [book["title"] for book in library["fiction"] if book["copies"]
> 2]
print(titles)
```

Ask ChatGPT things such as:

- *"Explain the list comprehension here."*
- *"What does `book["copies"] > 2` mean?"*
- *"Can you rewrite the code without list comprehension?"*

By doing this, you start to internalize how data moves through these structures, one conversation at a time.

The Secret Advantage

Understanding data structures is about building mental models. AI tools give you the power to test those models instantly. You can articulate your reasoning in simple terms and receive immediate feedback or corrections.

Instead of scrolling through Stack Overflow for hours or watching 20-minute YouTube explanations, you can ask *your specific question* and get context-aware guidance.

That does not mean you should let the AI do all the heavy lifting. You should still write, test, and break things yourself. However, when you encounter a mental block, whether it's due to deep nesting or vague errors, you have a co-pilot ready to simplify the chaos.

You do not have to be a genius to understand complex data structures. You only need the right kind of explanations, simple, visual, and in your language. With ChatGPT, that is precisely what you get.

Absolutely! Let us craft this sub-section to feel practical, human, and relatable—such as a senior developer mentoring a curious learner.

Improving Code Readability (Comments, Docstrings, and Naming Conventions)

Imagine opening a file that you wrote six months ago and immediately thinking:

> "*Who even wrote this?! Did I understand anything back then?*"

If you are honest, such an experience has happened to every developer at some point. Now, imagine someone else, a colleague, a client, or even future-you, has to touch your code. Readability becomes not just a nice-to-have but also a professional responsibility.

Readable code is easier to debug, simpler to extend, and less stressful to revisit. It is the difference between the following:

```
def f(x):
    return x**2 + 2*x + 1
```

...versus:

```
def calculate_quadratic(x):
    """
    Calculate the value of the quadratic equation: x^2 + 2x + 1.

    Parameters:
    x (int or float): The variable of the equation

    Returns:
    int or float: Result of the equation
    """
    return x**2 + 2*x + 1
```

The second snippet immediately communicates *intent*, even to someone unfamiliar with the formula. That is where ChatGPT becomes a valuable partner.

Using AI to Generate Meaningful Comments

Comments are small notes in code that explain *why* something exists, not just what it does. Many beginners make the mistake of writing obvious comments, such as:

```
i = 0  # set i to zero
```

Instead, you want comments that provide context:

```
i = 0  # counter for iterating over each row in the sales dataset
```

With ChatGPT, you can paste your code and ask:

"Suggest meaningful comments for this script."

It will not only annotate your logic but also often suggest clarifications that even experienced developers might overlook.

Crafting Docstrings

Docstrings are like mini user manuals for functions, classes, or modules. They are the difference between a confusing black box and a self-explanatory tool.

For instance, consider a function that filters email addresses:

```
def filter_emails(email_list):
    return [email for email in email_list if "@" in email]
```

Ask ChatGPT to generate a docstring, and you might get:

```
def filter_emails(email_list):
    """
    Filters a list of strings, returning only valid email addresses
containing '@'.

    Parameters:
    email_list (list of str): A list of strings to filter

    Returns:
    list of str: Only the strings that are valid email addresses
    """
    return [email for email in email_list if "@" in email]
```

Now, anyone, including future-you, can understand the function's purpose without tracing every line. Over time, this habit creates a readable codebase that others (and you) will thank you for.

Naming Conventions

Variable and function names are like the labels on ingredients in a kitchen. Ambiguous labels lead to confusion:

```
x = 5
y = 10
z = x + y
```

Better names convey meaning at a glance:

```
apples = 5
oranges = 10
total_fruit = apples + oranges
```

ChatGPT can review your code and suggest improvements for naming conventions, helping your variables, functions, and classes speak for themselves.

Real-World Example

Suppose, you inherited this function:

```
def f(lst):
    r = []
    for i in lst:
        if i%2==0:
            r.append(i*2)
    return r
```

It works, but readability is low. With ChatGPT, you could ask:

> *"Suggest improvements for naming, comments, and a docstring."*

It might return:

```
def double_even_numbers(numbers):
    """
    Returns a new list containing only the even numbers from the input
list,
    each multiplied by 2.

    Parameters:
    numbers (list of int): List of integers to process

    Returns:
    list of int: Doubled values of even numbers
    """
    doubled_evens = []
    for number in numbers:
        if number % 2 == 0:
            doubled_evens.append(number * 2)
    return doubled_evens
```

Notice the clarity—now anyone reading the code immediately knows what it does, why it exists, and how to use it.

Consistency over Cleverness

Readable code is consistent, not clever. ChatGPT can help enforce consistency by reviewing multiple functions at once and suggesting uniform styles for:

- Comments,
- Docstrings,
- Variable Naming, and
- Function Formatting.

This is especially valuable in team projects or large codebases where different developers may have different habits.

Building a Readable Mindset

The ultimate goal is not to rely on ChatGPT forever. It is to *internalize readability habits*:

- Always ask yourself: "Would someone else understand this without me here?"
- Use comments to explain *why*, not *what*.
- Write docstrings that serve as mini-manuals.
- Give names that describe the essence, not the type.

When you combine these habits with AI support, your code becomes easy to follow, easy to maintain, and far more professional.

AI as a Tool for Enforcing Python Best Practices (PEP 8 Compliance, Modularity)

Writing Python code is one thing. Writing Python code that other developers can read, maintain, and extend is another.

Professional codebases thrive on standards, consistency, readability, and modularity. Without them, even simple projects can quickly turn into chaos that is impossible to debug or scale.

Best practices are the set of widely accepted conventions in Python that make your code cleaner and easier to maintain. The most prominent example is **PEP 8**, Python's style guide.

They do not prevent errors, make collaboration smoother, and improve long-term project health.

Using AI to Ensure PEP 8 Compliance

PEP 8 covers things such as the following:

- Indentation (4 spaces per level),
- Naming conventions for variables, functions, and classes,
- Line length (generally 79 characters),
- Proper spacing around operators and after commas, and
- Consistent use of quotes.

Even experienced developers can slip. AI can act as a real-time reviewer, spotting deviations and suggesting corrections.

For example, consider this snippet:

```
def addTwoNumbers(a,b):
 return a+b
```

Ask ChatGPT:

> "*Rewrite this function according to* PEP 8 *standards*."

You might get:

```
def add_two_numbers(a, b):
    return a + b
```

Notice the subtle but meaningful changes:

- **`Snake_case`** for function name,
- Spaces after commas and operators, and
- Proper indentation.

This makes your code instantly more readable and professional.

Encouraging Modularity

Modular code means breaking your program into small, self-contained pieces, functions, classes, and modules, each responsible for a single task.

Why? Because:

- It is easier to test and debug.
- It promotes code reuse.
- It simplifies collaboration.

ChatGPT can help you refactor monolithic blocks into modular pieces. Consider this unstructured code:

```
data = [1, 2, 3, 4, 5]
total = 0
for num in data:
    total += num
average = total / len(data)
print("Average:", average)
```

Ask ChatGPT:

> *"Refactor this into a modular, reusable function."*

You may get:

```
def calculate_average(numbers):
    """
    Calculate the average of a list of numbers.

    Parameters:
    numbers (list of int or float): The list of numbers to average

    Returns:
    float: Average value
    """
    return sum(numbers) / len(numbers)

data = [1, 2, 3, 4, 5]
average = calculate_average(data)
print("Average:", average)
```

Now, the logic is reusable and self-contained. You can call **`calculate_average`** anywhere in your project, and your codebase is easier to read and maintain.

Structuring Larger Projects

Beyond individual functions, AI can guide you on project-level organization:

- Which functions should be grouped into classes?
- How to separate code into modules for better maintainability?
- How to structure directories for clarity?

For instance, in a web scraping project, ChatGPT can suggest the following:

```
project/
├── main.py              # Entry point
├── requirements.txt     # Project dependencies
├── scraper/             # Scraping logic
│   ├── __init__.py
│   ├── fetcher.py       # Handles HTTP requests
```

```
|   └── parser.py          # Extracts data from responses
├── utils/                 # Shared helper functions
├── inputs/                # Input URLs, configs, or seed files
├── outputs/               # Final scraped and processed data
├── data/                  # Raw or intermediate data
└── tests/                 # Unit tests
```

This kind of structure is not arbitrary; it enforces a mental model where each piece has a clear responsibility, reducing bugs and cognitive load.

Detecting Anti-Patterns

Even experienced developers can fall into traps such as the following:

- Long functions doing too many things,
- Copy-pasted code repeated across modules, and
- Overly nested loops or conditionals.

ChatGPT can flag these anti-patterns, suggest alternatives, and explain why a particular approach improves maintainability.

Example:

```
for i in range(len(data)):
    if data[i] % 2 == 0:
        print(data[i])
```

Prompt:

> *"Rewrite this to avoid anti-patterns and follow best practices."*

Result:

```
for number in data:
    if number % 2 == 0:
        print(number)
```

The improvement is subtle but important: cleaner iteration, easier readability, and better adherence to Pythonic conventions.

Building a Habit of Best Practices

AI is not replacing your judgment; it is reinforcing good habits. Over time, you will start recognizing:

- When your code strays from style guides,
- How to break large problems into smaller and testable modules, and
- The subtle impact of naming, spacing, and docstrings.

Using AI to Summarize and Refactor Legacy

Every developer eventually encounters legacy code that is messy code written by someone (or sometimes even by themselves) months or years ago. It may work, but understanding it is a puzzle, variable names make no sense, functions are too long, and comments are missing or misleading.

Legacy code is frustrating because you cannot just "replace it with a new version"; other parts of the system depend on it. Refactoring it requires clarity, patience, and a methodical approach.

Summarizing Messy Codebases

Before you refactor, you need to understand what is happening. Large scripts or modules can be overwhelming. AI can help by producing *concise summaries* of functions, classes, and workflows.

For example, consider a legacy script that processes sales data:

```
def process_data(data):
    temp = []
    for i in data:
        if i[2] > 100:
            temp.append(i)
    result = {}
    for row in temp:
        if row[0] not in result:
            result[row[0]] = []
        result[row[0]].append(row[2])
    return result
```

You might ask ChatGPT:

> "*Explain this function in plain English.*"

It could respond:

- Filters the rows in the `data` where the third column is greater than 100.
- Groups the filtered values by the first column.
- Returns a dictionary where keys are the first column values and values are lists of the third column numbers.

This gives you an instant overview without manually tracing every loop and index.

Refactoring Step by Step

Once you understand the logic, the next step is refactoring, making it more readable and maintainable. AI can guide you by suggesting:

- Clearer function and variable names,
- Using Python built-in functions or comprehensions for brevity, and
- Modularizing the code into reusable pieces.

For the above example, a refactored version could look like this:

First, let us walk through this problem in two stages.

We will start with a beginner-friendly approach, then refactor it using more advanced Python features.

The beginner version only uses:

- `for` loops,
- `if` statements, and
- Regular dictionaries.

These are core Python concepts every beginner should master.

```
def filter_and_group_sales(data, threshold=100):
    """
    Filters rows with sales above a threshold and groups sales by
product ID.

    Parameters:
    data (list of lists): Each row contains [product_id, date, sales_amount]
    threshold (int): Minimum sales amount to include

    Returns:
    dict: Keys are product IDs, values are lists of sales amounts
    """
    grouped_sales = {}

    for row in data:
        product_id = row[0]
        sales_amount = row[2]

        if sales_amount > threshold:
            if product_id not in grouped_sales:
                grouped_sales[product_id] = []
            grouped_sales[product_id].append(sales_amount)

    return grouped_sales
```

What is Happening Here

- Loop through each row in the data.
- Check if the sales amount is above the threshold.
- Group sales amounts by **product_id**.
- Create dictionary entries only when needed.

This version is explicit and easy to follow, making it ideal for beginners.

Once you are comfortable with the basics, Python offers tools that make this logic more concise.

```
from collections import defaultdict

def filter_and_group_sales(data, threshold=100):
    grouped_sales = defaultdict(list)

    for product_id, _, sales_amount in filter(lambda row: row[2] >
threshold, data):
        grouped_sales[product_id].append(sales_amount)

    return dict(grouped_sales)
```

What Changed and Why

- **Defaultdict(list)**: Automatically creates a list for each new key, removing manual checks.
- **Lambda + filter()**: Filters rows before processing, reducing nesting.
- **Tuple Unpacking**: Improves readability when working with structured data.

This version is shorter and more expressive, but it assumes familiarity with functional programming concepts.

Now, the function is more readable, modular, and self-documenting. The logic is clear, and any developer can pick it up quickly.

Identifying Redundant or Dead Code

Messy code often contains unused variables, functions that are never called, or repeated logic. Manually identifying these can take hours.

You can ask ChatGPT:

> *"Check this code for unused variables or redundant logic and suggest improvements."*

It will point out:

- Variables that are declared but never used,
- Loops that can be simplified, and

- Duplicate blocks of code that can be combined.

This not only cleans the code but also reduces the potential bugs and performance issues.

Rewriting Legacy Functions Efficiently

Some legacy functions are functional but overly complex. AI can help break them down into smaller and testable units.

Example:

```
def complex_function(data):
    result = []
    for i in data:
        if i[0] % 2 == 0:
            temp = i[1] * 2
            if temp > 10:
                result.append(temp)
    return result
```

Prompt ChatGPT:

"Refactor this into a readable and modular function with comments and docstring."

Result:

```
def process_even_values(data):
    """
    Processes even numbers in the dataset by doubling the second value and
    keeping only results greater than 10.

    Parameters:
    data (list of tuples): Each tuple contains (number, value)

    Returns:
    list: Processed values
    """
    processed = []
    for number, value in data:
        if number % 2 == 0:
            doubled_value = value * 2
            if doubled_value > 10:
                processed.append(doubled_value)
    return processed
```

The code is now self-explanatory, and future modifications will be easier and safer.

Building Confidence with Gradual Refactoring

The beauty of AI-assisted refactoring is not that it does the work for you, but that it lets you experiment safely. You can:

- Ask ChatGPT to suggest improvements,
- Compare the original and refactored code, and
- Learn patterns for better readability and efficiency.

Over time, you develop an instinct for spotting messy patterns, simplifying logic, and documenting effectively.

Legacy Project Rescue

Imagine joining a project with thousands of lines of Python code, unclear variable names, no docstrings, and no unit tests.

Using ChatGPT, you can:

1. Summarize each module to understand its purpose.
2. Identify repeated or redundant code blocks.
3. Suggest naming improvements and docstrings.
4. Refactor functions step by step, keeping functionality intact.
5. Introduce modularization for easier future maintenance.

This transforms a daunting codebase into one that is understandable, maintainable, and scalable, a skill highly valued in real-world development roles.

Hands-on Exercises: Feeding Real-World Open-Source Snippets into AI for Explanation and Optimization

Reading about code improvement is helpful, but *doing it* is where the learning sticks. The best way to gain confidence in understanding and refining Python code is to work with real-world examples. Open-source projects are perfect for this because they contain authentic, messy, and diverse code, just like you will encounter in professional environments.

By feeding these snippets into ChatGPT, you can explore:

- How functions and classes operate,
- What variables represent and why, and
- How to improve readability and structure.

Selecting Open-Source Snippets

Start small:

- Pick a function or class from a GitHub repository.
- Avoid extremely large files initially.
- Focus on projects that align with your learning goals (for example, data processing, automation, and web scraping).

Example snippet from a hypothetical GitHub project that calculates sales metrics:

```
def calc_metrics(data):
    total_sales = 0
    high_value = []
    for row in data:
        total_sales += row['amount']
        if row['amount'] > 1000:
            high_value.append(row)
    avg = total_sales / len(data)
    return total_sales, avg, high_value
```

Asking for an Explanation

Feed this code into ChatGPT and ask:

> "*Explain what this function does in plain English.*"

You might get a response like:

- Sums all sales amounts from `data`.
- Creates a list of transactions exceeding 1000 units.
- Computes the average sale amount.
- Returns total sales, average, and high-value transactions.

This step improves clarity, eliminating the need to trace each line manually.

Optimizing the Snippet

Once you understand the logic, ask ChatGPT:

> "*Suggest improvements for readability, structure, and efficiency.*"

A possible refactor:

```
def calculate_sales_metrics(transactions):
    """
    Calculate total sales, average sales, and identify high-value
transactions.
```

```
    Parameters:
    transactions (list of dict): Each dict contains sales info with key
'amount'

    Returns:
    tuple: total sales (float), average sale (float), list of high-value
transactions (list)
    """
    total_sales = sum(tx['amount'] for tx in transactions)
    high_value_transactions = [tx for tx in transactions if tx['amount']
> 1000]
    average_sales = total_sales / len(transactions) if transactions else 0
    return total_sales, average_sales, high_value_transactions
```

Improvements made:

- Clearer function name and variable names.
- Added docstring for context.
- Used list comprehension and `sum()` for brevity and readability, and
- Handled empty input gracefully.

Experimenting with Multiple Snippets

Repeat the process with snippets from different open-source projects:

- A small web scraper,
- A data cleaning function, and
- A utility for file parsing.

For each:

1. Understand the snippet's purpose.
2. Ask for suggestions to improve structure and readability.
3. Compare your own insights with ChatGPT's guidance.

Over time, you will start spotting patterns and understanding code without relying on AI as much. The AI acts as a mirror; it reflects areas you might miss and accelerates comprehension.

Lessons from Real-World Code

Working with real open-source code introduces several valuable lessons:

- **Diverse Coding Styles:** Not every developer follows the same conventions; exposure teaches adaptability.

- **Edge Cases:** Real-world code often includes checks for uncommon situations, helping you anticipate and handle them.
- **Performance Considerations:** Many snippets have subtle optimizations or inefficiencies you can learn from.
- **Collaborative Mindset:** Open-source code is inherently collaborative. Understanding and refactoring it mirrors team development practices.

Building a Practice Routine

To get the most out of this approach:

1. **Daily Snippets:** Pick one small snippet per day to analyze.
2. **Document Changes:** Keep a notebook of refactorings and insights.
3. **Compare Multiple Approaches:** See how different developers solve the same problem.
4. **Reflect on AI Suggestions:** Decide which recommendations truly improve your understanding.

This routine builds not just technical skills but also critical thinking and judgment, which are key traits of a professional developer.

Conclusion

Understanding Python code is an essential skill for programmers at all levels. With the aid of AI, tasks that once took hours, such as code explanation, debugging, and summarization, can now be completed in minutes.

In this chapter, you learned how to use AI as a powerful companion for understanding Python code, not just writing it. We explored how AI can break down syntax, logic, algorithms, and unfamiliar codebases in a simplified way.

In the next chapter, we will explore the art of breaking down complex programming problems into smaller, manageable parts and then translating them into effective prompts for AI.

Points to Remember

- PEP 8 and modularity are not arbitrary—they are about readability, maintainability, and collaboration.
- AI can act as a patient reviewer, suggesting improvements for style, structure, and organization.

- Refactoring messy code into functions, classes, and modules helps you work smarter and scale your projects.
- Over time, following AI-guided best practices develops your instinct for clean, professional code.
- Legacy or messy code is unavoidable, but understanding and improving it is a skill. AI acts as a guide to summarize, explain, and refactor code, making the process faster and safer.
- Refactoring is not just about "cleaning up"—it is about readability, modularity, and maintainability.
- Over time, learning from AI-assisted refactoring teaches you patterns and best practices that make you a stronger developer.

Key Terms

- **Artificial Intelligence (AI)**: The simulation of human intelligence in machines that are programmed to think, learn, and perform tasks.
- **Machine Learning (ML)**: A subset of AI that enables systems to learn from data without explicit programming.
- **Python Interpreter**: A program that reads and executes Python code line by line.
- **Code Parsing**: The process of analyzing code to understand its structure, syntax, and semantics.
- **Natural Language Processing (NLP)**: A branch of AI that helps computers understand, interpret, and generate human language.
- **Code Summarization**: The AI-assisted generation of human-readable explanations for code functionality.
- **Debugging**: The process of identifying and fixing errors or bugs in code.
- **Syntax Highlighting**: Visual differentiation of code elements to improve readability.
- **Code Refactoring**: The process of restructuring code without changing its external behavior to improve readability or efficiency.
- **AI Code Assistant**: An AI-powered tool that helps programmers write, understand, and improve codes.

Chapter 3 Problem Decomposition and Prompt Engineering

Introduction

If there is one invisible skill that separates *average coders* from *brilliant engineers*, it is not how many languages they know; it is how well they can think through problems. In the age of AI-assisted coding, that skill has a new name: problem decomposition.

When you strip away all the hype about "prompt engineering", what is really at the heart of it is the ability to break down big, messy problems into smaller, logical steps—steps so clear that even a machine can comprehend them.

This chapter will show you how to speak the language of logic that both humans and machines understand. You will learn how to take a vague idea and carve it into manageable parts. Amongst other things, you will write prompts that are specific enough to get high-quality results.

Structure

In this chapter, we will cover the following topics:

- Introduction to Problem Decomposition
    - Why Problem Decomposition Matters
    - Understanding How AI Thinks
    - From Big Idea to Working Prototype
    - Checklist: Signs You Have Properly Decomposed a Problem
- The Link between Decomposition and Effective Prompt Writing
    - Why Decomposition and Prompting are Two Sides of the Same Coin
    - Overwhelming versus Organized
    - The Anatomy of an Effective Prompt: A Realistic Prompt Chain

    - The "Conversation" Principle
    - Common Mistakes to Avoid
- Structuring Prompts with Context, Constraints, and Goals
    - Context: The Story Behind the Code
    - Constraints: The Boundaries That Shape Good Output
    - Goals: Defining What "Done" Looks Like
    - The CCG Framework
    - Practical Exercise
- Examples of Prompt-Driven Workflows for Data Analysis, Automation, and Web Tasks
    - Data Analysis Workflow: Exploring CSV Files
    - Automation Workflow
    - Pulling Data from an API
- Turning a Vague Request into a Working Program through Stepwise AI Collaboration
    - Understanding a Vague Request
    - Bringing It All Together

Introduction to Problem Decomposition

If you ask any experienced developer what they really do all day, they will not tell you, "I write code." They will probably say something closer to, "I spend half my day figuring out what the real problem is."

That is because writing code is not the hard part anymore; thinking clearly is. And nowhere does this become more obvious than when you start working with AI.

Why Problem Decomposition Matters

Think about the last time you faced a complex task, maybe something like:

> "*Build a script that automates daily sales reporting for three regions and emails the summary to the team.*"

It sounds simple until you try to do it all at once. Then you realize it is not one problem; it is *five or six smaller ones* hiding under a single sentence.

To tackle that properly, you would break it down like this:

1. Fetch sales data from each region (API, CSV, or database).

2. Clean and combine the datasets.
3. Calculate daily summaries and key metrics.
4. Format the results into a readable report.
5. Send the email automatically.

Each of these is now a separate problem you can feed to ChatGPT with clarity. You could even write a small prompt for each step, one that is easy to test, debug, and improve.

That is decomposition—the art of untangling complexity. It is what lets you and your AI assistant think together effectively.

Understanding How AI Thinks

ChatGPT does not actually "understand" problems the way humans do. It relies entirely on how clearly you describe what you want.

If your request is vague, it gives vague results.

If your goal is layered and unstructured, it gets lost halfway through.

But when you organize your problem into logical steps, you give the AI a structure to follow—a mental map that turns chaos into progress.

Here is an example.

Vague Prompt:

> *"Create a Python app that analyzes user feedback and finds trends."*

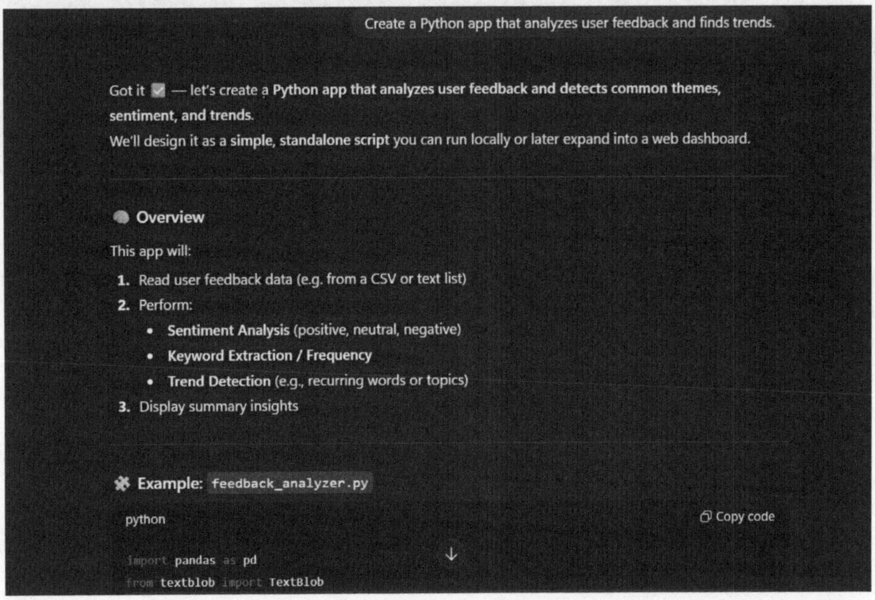

Figure 3.1: *ChatGPT Vague Prompt*

Decomposed Version:

"1. *Write Python code to load a CSV file of user feedback.*
2. *Identify the most common themes or keywords in the feedback.*
3. *Display the results as a summary table.*"

Notice how the second version reads such as a checklist. Now, ChatGPT can work through it systematically, generating functional, modular code for each part. You can even refine or replace steps without starting over.

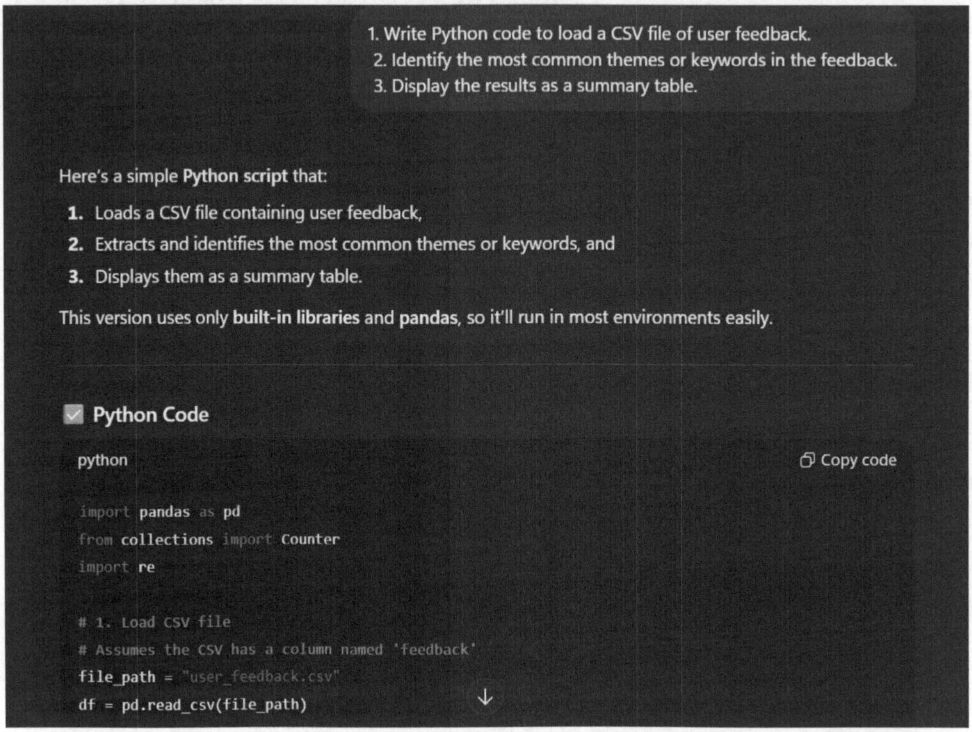

Figure 3.2: *ChatGPT Vague Prompt*

Decomposition is not just for machines; it is for your brain, too. It gives you a roadmap so you do not drown in details before you start.

From Big Idea to Working Prototype

Let us make it concrete with an example. Say your goal is to create a chatbot that helps users calculate their carbon footprint.

You could decompose it like this:

1. Gather user data (energy use, transportation habits, and so on).
2. Estimate emissions for each category.

3. Calculate total footprint.
4. Display suggestions to reduce emissions.
5. Save the user session and results.

Now, you can work with ChatGPT to build each block individually:

- One prompt for collecting user data,
- One for emission calculation logic, and
- Another for report formatting.

Instead of giving ChatGPT a single, overwhelming prompt, you are guiding it through a sequence, almost like pair programming with a teammate.

Checklist: Signs You Have Properly Decomposed a Problem

Before you move forward with any project, run through this quick checklist:

- Each step can be explained in a single sentence.
- You can test each part independently.
- You can describe the inputs and outputs for every step.
- You can reorder or replace a step without breaking everything else.
- You can ask ChatGPT to handle one piece at a time without confusion.

If you can do all five, your problem is decomposed well enough to work effectively with AI.

Problem decomposition is not about dumbing things down; it is about clarity. When you decompose a task, you are not simplifying your thinking; you are *sharpening* it. It is the same principle behind great engineering, writing, or design: the clearer the structure, the stronger the outcome.

And once you start seeing your projects this way, you will notice something powerful: AI stops being a mysterious tool and starts behaving like a true collaborator.

The Link between Decomposition and Effective Prompt Writing

When most people start using ChatGPT for coding, they focus on *what to ask*. But here is a reality seasoned developers quickly discover: how you ask matters just as much as what you ask.

The bridge between a great idea and a great AI response is *problem decomposition.* When you learn to break your task into pieces, writing strong prompts becomes natural, almost effortless.

Why Decomposition and Prompting are Two Sides of the Same Coin

Think of prompt writing as giving directions to someone who has never seen your project before.

If you hand them a full novel and say, "*Make it better,*" they will probably stare blankly at you.

But if you hand them one chapter and say, "*Improve the pacing in this section, keep the tone serious, but cut unnecessary sentences.*"

They can actually do something useful.

That is exactly how AI works.

When you decompose a problem, each smaller part becomes an individual prompt that the AI can understand, reason about, and respond to with precision. Instead of one big, blurry request, you are giving it a clear sequence of micro-tasks that lead to a larger goal.

Let us look at an example. Feel free to try it out on your ChatGPT app.

Overwhelming versus Organized

Vague Prompt:

> "*Build a data visualization dashboard using Python.*"

ChatGPT might return something overly simplified, maybe a single `matplotlib` graph with dummy data.

Decomposed Prompts:

- "*Generate Python code that loads a CSV of sales data into a pandas DataFrame.*"
- "*Create functions to calculate monthly sales growth and regional performance.*"
- "*Generate code that visualizes both metrics using Plotly with an interactive layout.*"
- "*Add a simple web interface with Streamlit to display the visualizations.*"

Now, you are giving ChatGPT clear boundaries on what each step does, what inputs it handles, and what output to expect.

Instead of hallucinating a "complete dashboard," it now acts like a junior developer who follows your architecture.

That is the power of decomposition-driven prompting: it creates structure in what would otherwise be chaos.

The Anatomy of an Effective Prompt

When you have decomposed a problem, writing a high-quality prompt becomes a repeatable pattern.

Here is a simple structure you can use every time:

- **Context**: What you are trying to achieve and why.

  "*I am building a web scraper to collect product prices from e-commerce websites.*"

- **Task**: What the AI should do specifically.

  "*Write a Python function using BeautifulSoup that extracts product names and prices.*"

- **Constraints**: Any rules or limits.

  "*Ensure the code handles missing prices gracefully and uses requests, not Selenium.*"

- **Goal**: What the final output should look like.

  "*Return a list of dictionaries with keys:* `name`, `price`, *and* `url`."

When you get used to structuring prompts this way, you will notice two things:

- The AI starts producing more accurate and maintainable code.
- You start thinking more clearly, and your decomposition naturally trains you to communicate with precision.

A Realistic Prompt Chain

Let us say you want ChatGPT to build a Python CLI tool that renames files in bulk.

You could break it into three prompts:

1. **Prompt 1 (Setup):**

   "*Generate Python code that reads all file names in a given folder using* **`os.listdir()`**."

2. **Prompt 2 (Logic):**

   "*Add logic that renames files based on a pattern like* `newname_1.jpg`, `newname_2.jpg`, *and so on.*"

3. **Prompt 3 (Safety):**

    "Update the script to confirm before renaming files and create a log of all renamed files."

Each stage is small, testable, and clear.

This is decomposition feeding directly into your prompt design.

You are not just getting code; you are building a workflow where AI becomes part of your thinking loop.

The "Conversation" Principle

A good prompt is not a command; it is a collaboration. Decomposition helps you think in conversations rather than monologues.

For example:

> "ChatGPT, *here is my function for generating reports. It works, but the runtime is slow. Can you suggest optimizations?*"

That is not an order; it is an invitation for feedback. When you start treating AI like a partner instead of a black box, your prompts become richer, and your results become more human.

Common Mistakes to Avoid

Even experienced developers fall into these traps:

- **Asking Everything at Once.**
  Break your goal into smaller and testable prompts.
- **Skipping Context.**

  Always give background, what the code is for, who will use it, and what matters most.
- **Ignoring Iteration.**

  Do not expect perfect results the first time. Refine, test, and clarify until it fits your needs.
- **Overloading with Jargon.**

  Keep prompts plain and natural. The AI understands clean, direct language better than buzzwords.

- **Emotional Prompting.**

  Yes, this happens more often than you think. Learners frustrated with errors often use emotional language like:

  "Why can you not just get it right?"

  "This is not what I meant!"

Once you connect decomposition to prompting, you will notice a shift:

You stop feeling like you are *using* an AI tool and start feeling like you are *leading* one.

Your prompts will sound like the instructions you would give a colleague.

You will move faster, make fewer mistakes, and finally start building projects that feel deliberate and not accidental.

Structuring Prompts with Context, Constraints, and Goals

If problem decomposition is about breaking things down, then prompt structuring is about building them back up.

Think of it as giving your AI assistant a map, where to start, what to avoid, and what the destination should look like.

A prompt without these three—context, constraints, and goals—is like sending a junior developer to "just build something cool." You will get something, but probably not what you had in mind.

So, let us unpack these three pieces and see how they shape the way we talk to ChatGPT in a developer's workflow.

Context: The Story behind the Code

Every good collaboration starts with a background.

When you tell ChatGPT to "optimize this code," it does not know *why* it exists. Is it for a web app, a data pipeline, or a school project? That missing story often leads to confusing or unusable output.

Context answers the "why."

Here is a simple example:

❌ *"Write Python code to calculate discounts."*

✅ *"I am building an online store where users can apply seasonal discount codes. Write a Python function that calculates the final price after applying discounts and taxes."*

Notice the difference?

With context, ChatGPT now understands the use case, user flow, and business logic, which means it can produce cleaner, more relevant code.

When giving context, include:

- The purpose of the task,
- The environment (CLI, web app, API, and so on), and
- Any user interactions or data sources involved.

In short, treat the AI as a teammate joining your project midstream; fill them in before they touch the keyboard.

Constraints: The Boundaries That Shape Good Output

Constraints tell ChatGPT what not to do, which is often more important than what to do. Without constraints, you will get broad, sometimes overcomplicated code that looks nice but does not fit your project.

Let us look at an example:

❌ *"Write a script to scrape job listings."*

✅ *"Write a Python script that scrapes job titles and links from a single webpage using BeautifulSoup.*

Do not use Selenium or APIs. Limit the code to under 40 lines."

Now you have drawn clear borders: what libraries to use, what limits to respect, and what is off the table.
This focus helps the AI stay efficient; you are not just telling it what to build, but how to think while building it.

Here are a few types of constraints you can include:

- **Technical:** Specific libraries, file structures, or runtime limits
- **Stylistic:** Naming conventions, indentation style, or docstring format
- **Performance:** Time complexity or memory usage
- **Practical:** File size, readability, or security restrictions

Remember, constraints do not restrict creativity; they guide it. A well-defined box can often lead to surprisingly innovative solutions.

Goals: Defining What "Done" Looks Like

Finally, every great prompt ends with a *goal*. It is the equivalent of saying, "*Here is what success looks like.*"

A goal can describe the expected output, user experience, or measurable outcome.

For example:

> "*Generate Python code that takes a CSV of expenses and produces a summary report showing total, average, and highest spending category formatted as a Markdown table.*"

The AI now knows exactly how to wrap things up; the format, structure, and content are all crystal clear.

To make your goals stronger:

- Be specific about output type (code, table, explanation, visualization, and so on).
- Mention formatting requirements, if any.
- Clarify success criteria: for example, "Code should run without external dependencies."

The clearer your goal, the easier it becomes to verify if the output is correct.

The CCG Framework

When you combine **Context + Constraints + Goals**, you get what is called the **CCG Framework,** a simple formula that can turn a weak prompt into a super-efficient one.

Example:

> "*I am building a small CLI tool that renames image files for photographers (context). Write Python code that renames files in a selected folder to follow the format* `wedding_001.jpg`, `wedding_002.jpg`, *and so on, using the* `os` *module (constraints).*
>
> *The script should print a confirmation message for each renamed file and handle duplicates safely (goal).*"

Each part builds upon the other background gives purpose, limits add clarity, and goals define success.

Practical Exercise

Let us practice turning a messy prompt into a structured one.

Original:

> "*Create a web scraper that gets prices of laptops from a site.*"

Structured (with CCG):

> *"I am creating a Python-based price tracker for an e-commerce comparison tool.*
>
> *Write a script using `requests` and `BeautifulSoup` that scrapes laptop names and prices from a single product page (context + constraint).*
>
> *The output should be a JSON list with keys `name`, `price`, and `link`, formatted cleanly and printed in the console (goal)."*

The second version leaves nothing to chance. It gives ChatGPT all the information it needs to act as your coding assistant, not your guesser.

Examples of Prompt-Driven Workflows for Data Analysis, Automation, and Web Tasks

You have learned how to break problems down and how to communicate clearly with your coding assistant.

Now it is time to put all that theory to work.

In this section, we will explore *real-world scenarios* where ChatGPT becomes a hands-on coding partner.

You will write prompts, review responses, install the right Python libraries in VS Code, and run working scripts that solve useful problems.

We will cover three workflows:

1. **Data Analysis:** Extracting insights from CSV files.
2. **Automation:** Performing repetitive file or system tasks automatically.
3. **Web Tasks:** Interacting with online data (such as scraping, API calls, or automating a simple web request).

Each workflow follows the CCG Framework you learned earlier:

- **C** – *Context*: What you are trying to do.
- **C** – *Constraints*: Any limits, formats, or data.
- **G** – *Goal*: The exact output or outcome you want.

You will also see how prompt wording and decomposition improve accuracy and how to debug or refine results as you go.

Data Analysis Workflow: Exploring CSV Files

Imagine you have received a sales report in CSV format and want to understand performance by region.

This is a common beginner-friendly scenario, perfect for practicing structured prompting.

Step 1: Set the Stage (Context)

Open your VS Code environment and ensure that Python is installed.

Create a new file named `sales_analysis.py`.

Before anything, install the required libraries by opening the **terminal** in VS Code and running:

```
pip install pandas matplotlib
```

These are the core tools for data manipulation and visualization.

Step 2: The Prompt

In ChatGPT, type this:

> You are my coding assistant. I have a file named **`sales_data.csv`** containing `region`, `sales`, and `month` columns.
>
> I want to write a Python script that loads the CSV using pandas, calculates total sales per region, and displays a bar chart.
>
> Please write the code with comments for clarity.

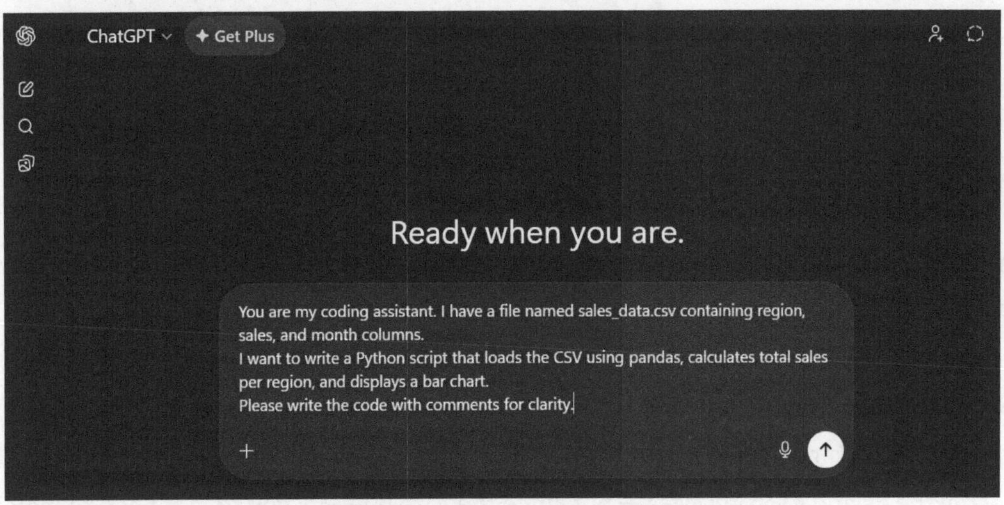

Figure 3.3: *ChatGPT Prompt*

Step 3: Analyze and Refine

You will likely get a script such as this:

```
import pandas as pd
import matplotlib.pyplot as plt

# Load the data
data = pd.read_csv('sales_data.csv')

# Ensure the sales column is numeric
data['sales'] = pd.to_numeric(data['sales'], errors='coerce')

# Remove rows with invalid or missing sales values
data = data.dropna(subset=['sales'])

# Group by region and sum sales
region_sales = data.groupby('region')['sales'].sum()

# Plot the data
region_sales.plot(kind='bar')
plt.title('Total Sales by Region')
plt.xlabel('Region')
plt.ylabel('Sales')
plt.show()
```

Step 4: Debug and Iterate

Now, imagine the dataset had missing values. You could refine your prompt like this:

> The code fails because of missing sales values. Update the code to ignore NaN values and show total sales for valid data only.

Within seconds, ChatGPT will respond with a cleaner version that handles errors.

Automation Workflow

Automation is one of Python's superpowers, and ChatGPT can make writing automation scripts effortless when you structure prompts properly.

Let us say you often need to **rename multiple files** in a folder to maintain consistency.

Step 1: Set the Stage (Context)

Open VS Code and create a new file named **`rename_files.py`**.

Install the `os` and `glob` libraries — but since they are built-in, you do not need to install anything extra this time.

Step 2: The Prompt

> I want to automate renaming all `.txt` files in a folder by adding today's date at the end of each filename.
>
> Write a Python script that loops through the folder, renames each file, and prints the new filename.
>
> The code should skip files that already have today's date in the name.

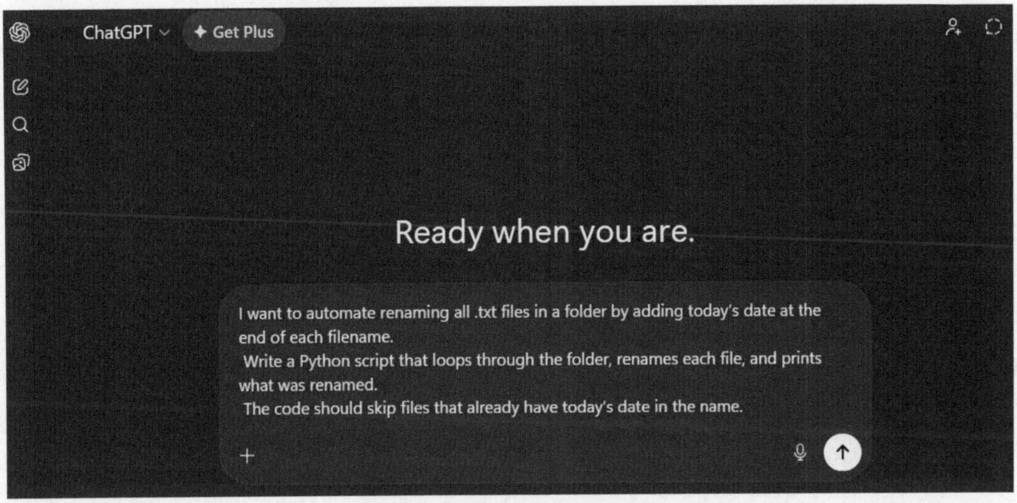

Figure 3.4: *ChatGPT Prompt*

Step 3: Review and Learn

ChatGPT might return this:

```
from pathlib import Path
from datetime import datetime

# Get today's date
today = datetime.now().strftime("%Y-%m-%d")

# Loop through all .txt files in the current directory
for file in Path(".").glob("*.txt"):
    stem = file.stem  # filename without extension

    # Check if filename already ends with today's date
    if not stem.endswith(today):
        new_name = f"{stem}_{today}{file.suffix}"
        file.rename(file.with_name(new_name))
        print(f"Renamed: {file.name} -> {new_name}")
    else:
        print(f"Skipped: {file.name}")
```

Pulling Data from an API

Before writing any code, it is important to understand what an API is and what you are allowed to do with it.

An API (Application Programming Interface) allows one program to request data or services from another program over the internet. In this case, your Python script will request live cryptocurrency prices from a public service.

CoinGecko is a popular platform that provides cryptocurrency market data, including prices, volumes, and market capitalization.

The CoinGecko API:

- Is public and free to use,
- Does not require an API key for basic endpoints, and
- Is commonly used for learning, prototypes, and small projects.

This makes it ideal for beginners experimenting with real-world data.

Who Can Use This API?

- Students and learners,
- Developers building prototypes or dashboards, and
- Anyone exploring cryptocurrency data programmatically.

No account or authentication is required for the endpoint used in this example.

Even free APIs come with constraints:

- **Rate limits** apply (too many requests in a short time may be blocked).
- Data is provided **as-is** and may not be perfectly accurate in real time.
- Not suitable for **high-frequency trading or production finance systems.**
- Internet connectivity is required.

Understanding these limitations helps you design scripts that behave responsibly.

Create a new file named **`crypto_prices.py`**.

You will need the requests library to make HTTP requests. Install it with:

```
pip install requests
```

Ask ChatGPT:

> Write a Python script that fetches the current Bitcoin and Ethereum prices from the CoinGecko API.
>
> `(https://api.coingecko.com/api/v3/simple/price?ids=bitcoin,ethereum&vs_currencies=usd).`

- Print the prices in a readable format.
- Add error handling in case the request fails.

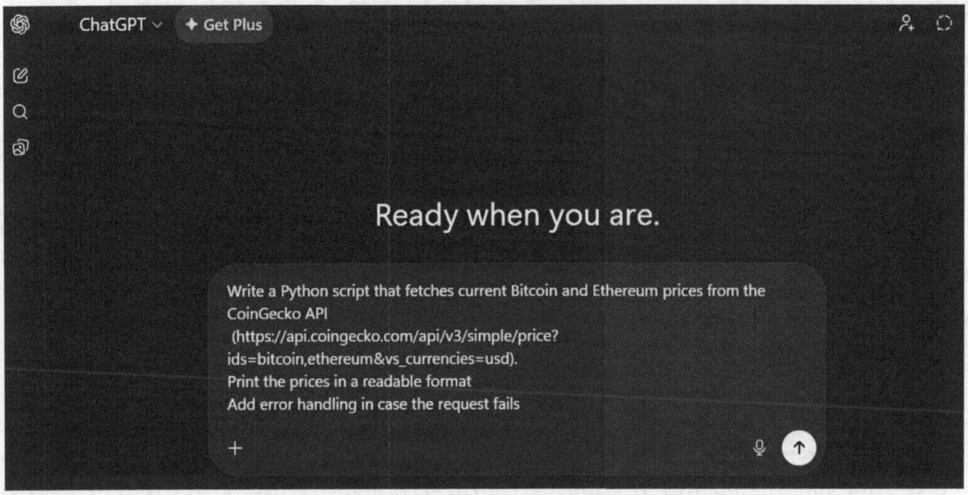

Figure 3.5: *ChatGPT Prompt*

Here is an example of what you might get:

```
import requests
url = "https://api.coingecko.com/api/v3/simple/
price?ids=bitcoin,ethereum&vs_currencies=usd"
try:
    response = requests.get(url)
    response.raise_for_status()
    data = response.json()

    print(f"Bitcoin: ${data['bitcoin']['usd']}")
    print(f"Ethereum: ${data['ethereum']['usd']}")
except requests.exceptions.RequestException as e:
    print("Error fetching prices:", e)
```

Run this script in VS Code, and you will see live cryptocurrency prices printed to the terminal.

Once your script works, try improving it using refinement prompts such as:

> Add timestamps to the output so I can track when prices were fetched.
>
> Format the output in a table-like display.
>
> Save the results to a CSV file for future reference.

Each prompt teaches you something new about modular programming and problem decomposition.

Turning a Vague Request into a Working Program through Stepwise AI Collaboration

Every developer has faced that moment when a client, boss, or colleague says something such as:

> "*Can you make a small tool that helps people calculate their monthly savings goal?*"

No detailed specs.

No clear inputs or outputs.

Just a random idea with no clear direction.

Now, before AI tools such as ChatGPT, this kind of request often meant several rounds of back-and-forth discussions, mockups, and trial-and-error coding. But today, you can take that vague idea and, through structured collaboration with ChatGPT, break it down into a fully functional Python program while understanding each decision made along the way.

Understanding a Vague Request

Let us imagine this situation:

You have been asked to "build a tool that helps users manage their personal expenses and savings."

That is all you get. No data. No structure. No previous codebase.

Here is what most beginners do:

They immediately rush to ChatGPT and type:

> "*Write me a Python expense tracker.*"

They also get a lengthy block of code they do not understand, which usually breaks on the first run.

AI gives its best when you give it structure.

That is where problem decomposition comes in. You do not ask for the entire house; you build it brick by brick.

Breaking down the Problem

Let us walk through how you can use ChatGPT effectively to solve this problem.

You start by defining what the final program should do, even if roughly.

Prompt:

> I want to build a small Python program that helps users track expenses and see how much they have saved each month. The program should store data and display summaries.

This gives ChatGPT a clear goal. You are not asking for code yet; you are framing the destination.

Now, you move one step deeper.

Prompt:

> Help me break this down into smaller steps. What features should I add first?

ChatGPT might respond with something such as:

1. Add a function to record an expense (amount, category, and date).
2. Store data in a CSV file.
3. Add a function to calculate total expenses and savings for the month.
4. Display a summary report.

Perfect.

You now have a project structure without writing a single line of code.

Start Building in Layers

Let us start with the first step: recording an expense.

Prompt:

> *Write a Python function that takes **`amount`**, **`category`**, and **`date`**, and appends them to a CSV file named **`expenses.csv`**.*

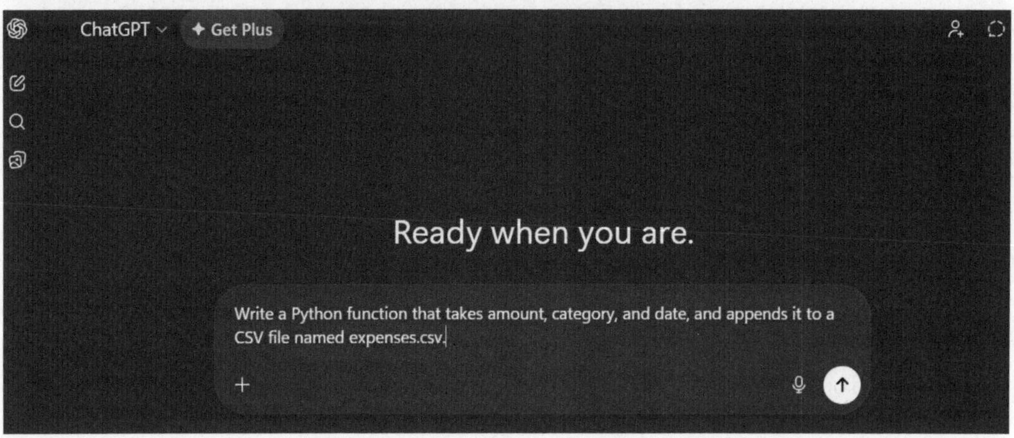

Figure 3.6: *ChatGPT Prompt*

ChatGPT might give you something such as this:

```
import csv

def add_expense(amount, category, date):
    try:
        with open('expenses.csv', mode='a', newline='') as file:
            writer = csv.writer(file)
            writer.writerow([amount, category, date])
        print("Expense added successfully!")
    except FileNotFoundError:
        print("No expenses recorded yet. Please add an expense first.")
    except Exception as e:
        print(f"An unexpected error occurred: {e}")
```

Ask for Explanations along the Way

One of the best ways to use ChatGPT is not just to generate code and move on, but also to understand.

Prompt:

> *Explain what each line of this code does, as if you are teaching a beginner.*

ChatGPT might walk you through each function, file operation, and parameter, helping you understand not only *what* happens, but also *why*.

Move to the Next Feature

Now, you want to analyze expenses.

Prompt:

> *Now write another function that reads the same* ***`expenses.csv`*** *file and calculates the total amount spent by category.*

The AI will generate something like this:

```
import csv
from collections import defaultdict

def summarize_expenses(currency_symbol=None):
    """
    Summarizes total expenses by category.

    Assumptions:
    - expenses.csv contains a header row: amount, category, date
    - amount values are numeric
```

```
    Parameters:
    currency_symbol (str | None): Optional currency symbol to prefix
totals
    """
    totals = defaultdict(float)

    try:
        with open('expenses.csv', mode='r', newline='') as file:
            reader = csv.DictReader(file)  # Explicitly handles header
row

            for row in reader:
                try:
                    amount = float(row['amount'])
                    category = row['category']
                    totals[category] += amount
                except (KeyError, ValueError):
                    # Skip rows with missing or invalid data
                    continue

        for category, total in totals.items():
            if currency_symbol:
                print(f"{category}: {currency_symbol}{total:,.2f}")
            else:
                print(f"{category}: {total:,.2f}")

    except FileNotFoundError:
        print("No expenses found. Please add expenses before
summarizing.")
```

Notice how each function stands alone, modular, reusable, and easy to test.

That is a key skill professional developers use daily.

Add Polishing Touches through Conversation

Once your code runs, do not stop there.

Talk to ChatGPT as if you are in a real design meeting:

> *The output looks plain. Can we make it display totals in descending order and highlight the category with the highest spending?*

You will likely get an improved version with sorting logic and conditional formatting added. Every question you ask makes the code more refined and personalized.

Bringing It All Together

By this stage, you have co-created a working expense tracker. Let us tie it together with a simple user menu.

Prompt:

> *Combine everything into a simple text-based menu so I can choose to add an expense, view a summary, or exit.*

ChatGPT's output might look like this:

```
def main():
    while True:
        print("\n--- Expense Tracker ---")
        print("1. Add Expense")
        print("2. View Summary")
        print("3. Exit")

        choice = input("Enter choice: ")

        if choice == "1":
            amount = input("Enter amount: ")
            category = input("Enter category: ")
            date = input("Enter date (YYYY-MM-DD): ")
            add_expense(amount, category, date)
        elif choice == "2":
            summarize_expenses()
        elif choice == "3":
            break
        else:
            print("Invalid choice. Try again.")

if __name__ == "__main__":
    main()
```

Now, you have a fully working CLI program—built step by step, with ChatGPT as a partner in thought.

Conclusion

When you first start working with AI tools such as ChatGPT for coding, it is easy to think that the magic lies in the tool itself. But as you have seen throughout this chapter, the real magic lies in how you think, how you break down a problem, structure your instructions, and refine your prompts.

Problem decomposition is not just a technical step; it is a way of teaching your mind to think like a builder. Once you master it, you will find that most of your coding frustrations fade away because every problem starts looking like a set of smaller, conquerable steps.

In the next chapter, we will explore one of the worst nightmares of many developers: debugging and refactoring with AI.

Points to Remember

- Break large problems into smaller and logical steps before prompting.
- Always start with clarity, define your context, constraints, and end goal.
- The quality of your prompt directly affects the accuracy and relevance of the response.
- Do not expect the first output to be perfect; iterate.
- Use comments and natural language in your prompts to give ChatGPT a clearer sense of direction.
- Avoid emotional or vague prompts such as "make this better"; instead, specify how and why you want it improved.
- Always test outputs locally on VS Code before finalizing.

Exercise

Try this process on a fresh problem.

Pick a vague idea, such as:

> "*Build a tool that helps users generate daily motivational quotes and saves them with timestamps.*"

Follow the same steps:

1. Define the goal.
2. Break down into smaller features.
3. Ask ChatGPT to generate one function at a time.
4. Test and refine.
5. Combine into a working program.

Libraries you might need:

```
pip install requests
```

(for fetching quotes from an API such as ZenQuotes or Quotable).

You will have a fully functional "quote tracker" that can fetch, store, and display quotes, all through structured collaboration.

Key Terms

- **Problem Decomposition:** Breaking down a complex task into smaller, manageable sub-tasks that are easier to implement and test.
- **Prompt Engineering:** The process of crafting structured, context-rich instructions that guide an AI tool toward useful and relevant outputs.
- **Context:** Background information or setup details that help AI understand *where* and *why* a problem exists.
- **Constraints:** Rules or limitations that define how a solution should behave, for example, using a specific library or avoiding global variables.
- **Iteration:** The process of revising, testing, and refining prompts or code to improve accuracy and performance.
- **Prompt Workflow:** A repeatable pattern of problem-solving that involves decomposition, prompting, reviewing, testing, and refining results.
- **Refinement Loop:** A cycle of adjusting both prompts and code outputs until the AI's response aligns with your intent and works as expected.

Chapter 4
Debugging and Refactoring with AI

Introduction

Every developer, at some point, faces that moment of panic in the editor, an unexpected error message, or a program that refuses to behave as intended.

Debugging has always been considered one of the most challenging and least glamorous parts of coding. Yet, it is also where developers improve their problem-solving skills, build resilience, and develop an intimate understanding of how code actually works.

Tools such as ChatGPT are no longer just helpers for writing code; they are partners in debugging and refactoring, capable of illuminating the blind spots that even experienced developers sometimes overlook.

In this chapter, we will explore the profound ways AI can transform the debugging process. You will learn to interpret cryptic error messages with AI's support, uncover logic flaws and runtime issues faster, and refactor code to make it cleaner, modular, and more maintainable. We will also explore the subtle art of verifying AI-generated fixes, because while AI can suggest solutions, human judgment ensures that they are correct, efficient, and aligned with your design intent.

Structure

In this chapter, we will cover the following topics:

- Using AI to Interpret Error Messages and Stack Traces
- Identifying Logic Errors, Runtime Issues, and Syntax Mistakes with AI Guidance
- Step-by-Step Debugging Workflows with AI
- AI-Assisted Code Refactoring: Cleaner Functions, Modularization, and DRY Principles

Using AI to Interpret Error Messages and Stack Traces

Let us imagine that you have spent an hour writing a Python script, anticipating your first successful run, and then a wall of red text floods your console.

```
Traceback (most recent call last):
  File "expense_tracker.py", line 12, in <module>
    add_expense("100", "Food", "2025-11-11")
  File "expense_tracker.py", line 5, in add_expense
    writer.writerow([amount, category, date])
TypeError: unsupported operand type(s) for +: 'int' and 'str'
```

Most beginners struggle at this point, unsure what went wrong or where to start. Even experienced developers sometimes need a moment to decode what the traceback is actually telling them. Understanding error messages and stack traces is crucial; they are Python's way of talking to you about what went wrong and where.

In this section, you will learn how to use ChatGPT as a collaborator in decoding errors—not just giving answers but helping you *understand* what each message means, why it happened, and how to prevent similar mistakes in the future.

Identifying the Error Type

The first step in debugging is always understanding the error type. Errors in Python are broadly divided into:

- **Syntax Errors:** Python cannot interpret your code because it breaks grammar rules.
- **Runtime Errors:** Your program starts running but encounters an issue during execution.
- **Logic Errors:** Code runs without crashing, but results are incorrect.

Let us revisit the example above:

```
TypeError: unsupported operand type(s) for +: 'int' and 'str'
```

Here is what is happening: Python is telling you the operation you tried is invalid. You are attempting to add an integer and a `string`.

Using ChatGPT to Clarify:

Prompt:

I ran this Python code and got `TypeError: unsupported operand type(s) for +: 'int' and 'str'`. Can you explain what this means in simple terms?

Figure 4.1: *ChatGPT Prompt*

ChatGPT can break it down like this:

Python cannot combine numbers and text directly. Somewhere in your code, you are trying to perform addition or concatenation between a number and a string. You need to convert types appropriately, for example, using **`int()`** or **`str()`**.

This turns a cryptic message into a digestible explanation and equips you to fix it yourself.

Tracing the Source of the Error

Next, you want to pinpoint where the error occurred. Stack traces provide a roadmap:

```
File "expense_tracker.py", line 12, in <module>
add_expense("100", "Food", "2025-11-11")
File "expense_tracker.py", line 5, in add_expense
writer.writerow([amount, category, date])
```

Here, you can see:

- The error happened in the function `add_expense`.
- The problematic line is **`writer.writerow([amount, category, date])`**.
- Python traced the issue back to your main script call (**`line 12`**).

ChatGPT can help you step through the stack by asking:

Can you walk me through this stack trace line by line and tell me which variable is causing the TypeError?

You will see explanations such as:

- `"amount"` is a string `"100"`.
- `writer.writerow` expects all items in the row to be compatible types (for example, strings or numbers in the right format).

- Therefore, convert `"100"` to an integer or float before writing.

Contextual Debugging Prompts

One of the most valuable ways to leverage ChatGPT here is by providing context around your code. Instead of simply pasting the error, you include:

- Relevant code snippets,
- What you expected to happen, and
- Any attempts you have already made.

Prompt example:

I am trying to record expenses in a CSV file with this function:

```
def add_expense(amount, category, date):

    with open('expenses.csv', mode='a', newline='') as file:
        writer = csv.writer(file)
        writer.writerow([amount, category, date])
```

I ran **`add_expense("100", "Food", "2025-11-11")`** and got a `TypeError`. How can I fix it, and why did it happen?

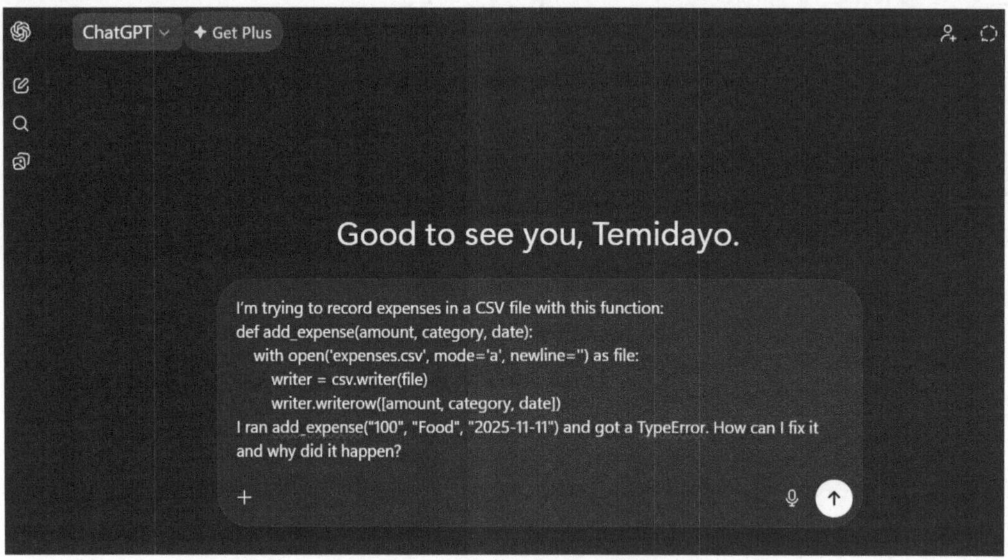

Figure 4.2: *ChatGPT Prompt*

The AI will typically respond with:

Convert the amount to a number before writing:

```
writer.writerow([float(amount), category, date])
```

The error occurred because Python does not allow mixing strings and numbers in arithmetic operations or certain function calls.

Why This Matters: You now not only fix the bug, but you understand the *root cause*, the exact mismatch between your data type and Python's expectations.

Spotting Subtle Runtime Issues

Some errors are trickier; they appear occasionally, depend on data, or involve multiple functions. Examples include:

- `IndexError`: Accessing an element that does not exist in a list.
- `KeyError`: Looking for a dictionary key that is not there.
- `AttributeError`: Calling a method on an object that does not have it.

AI can guide you through these, too. For instance, feeding ChatGPT both your function and sample input allows it to explain:

Your code works most of the time, but if **`expenses.csv`** is empty, the `for` loop will fail because the `reader` has no lines. Consider adding a check for an empty file.

By iterating this way, you learn to **think proactively about edge cases**.

Comparing Human versus AI Interpretation

- **Human Approach:** Read the error, Google it, look at docs, try a fix, test, repeat.
- **AI-assisted Approach:** Paste code + error + context, ask for explanation, fix, test, refine.

You still need human judgment to ensure fixes are correct, efficient, and do not introduce new issues. AI accelerates comprehension, but does not replace careful thinking.

Identifying Logic Errors, Runtime Issues, and Syntax Mistakes with AI Guidance

When your Python code does not crash but still produces the expected behavior, that is a logic error. When it refuses to run at all, that is a runtime or syntax issue.

And while traditional debugging tools such as **`pdb`** or print statements still work, using ChatGPT as a coding companion brings something extra: *contextual understanding*. You can show the code, and it not only points out the error but also explains *why* it is happening and how to fix it intelligently.

Let us explore each type of error step by step and how to diagnose them with AI.

Syntax Mistakes: The Basics

These are the easiest to spot but often the most annoying.

Example 1: Missing Colon

```
def greet(name)
    print(f"Hello, {name}!")
```

VS Code immediately complains:

```
SyntaxError: expected ':'
```

Using ChatGPT for Guidance:

Prompt:

I am getting a syntax error in this Python function. What am I missing?

```
def greet(name)
    print(f"Hello, {name}!")
```

ChatGPT might respond:

You forgot a colon (:) after the function definition. The correct version is:

```
def greet(name):
    print(f"Hello, {name}!")
```

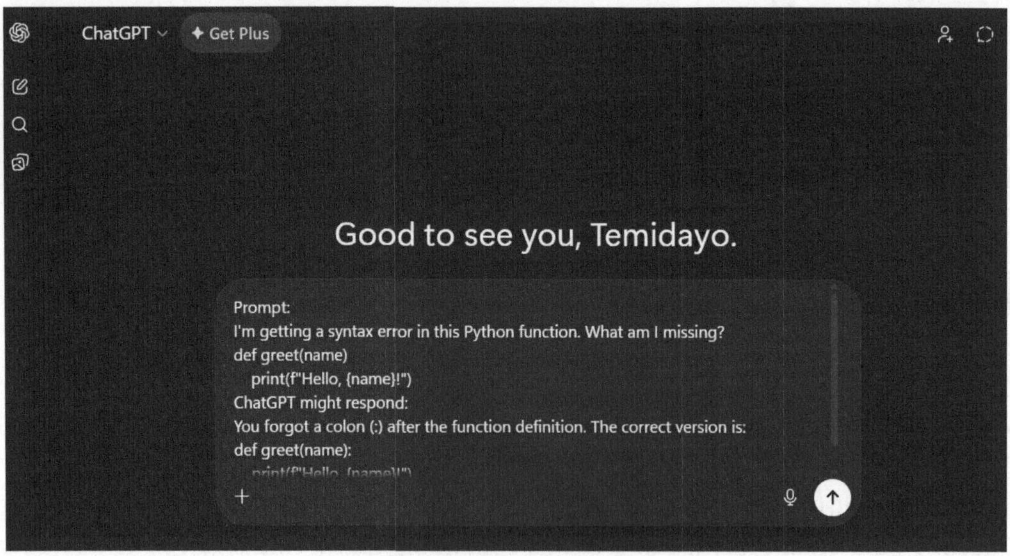

Figure 4.3: *ChatGPT Prompt*

Pretty simple, but it gets better when the syntax issue is buried deeper. For instance, inside a nested structure.

Example 2: Complex Syntax Error

```
data = [1, 2, 3, 4
print(sum(data))
```

You get:

```
SyntaxError: '(' was never closed
```

Prompt:

Can you help me find the syntax issue in this code?

```
data = [1, 2, 3, 4
print(sum(data))
```

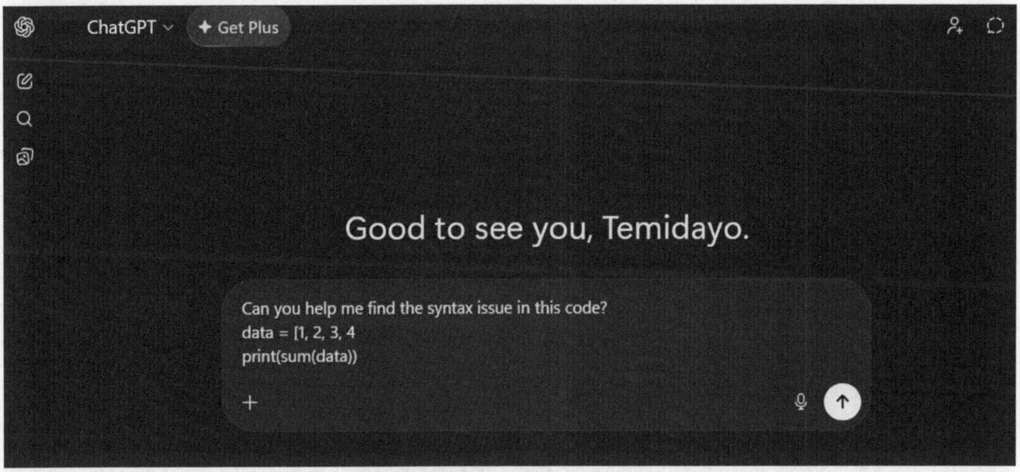

Figure 4.4: *ChatGPT Prompt*

ChatGPT:

There is a missing closing bracket in the list definition. It should be:

```
data = [1, 2, 3, 4]
print(sum(data))
```

You will notice the AI does not just fix the syntax; it explains what *caused* the problem. That is how you build debugging intuition.

Runtime Errors: When Your Code Breaks Midway

These are the ones that appear only *after* you run your code. AI is surprisingly effective here because it can read both your code and the *error message* and reason through possible causes.

Example: Division by Zero

```
def calculate_average(numbers):
    return sum(numbers) / len(numbers)
print(calculate_average([]))
```

Error:

```
ZeroDivisionError: division by zero
```

Prompt:

Here is my function:

```
def calculate_average(numbers):
    return sum(numbers) / len(numbers)
print(calculate_average([]))
What is causing the ZeroDivisionError, and how can I prevent it?
```

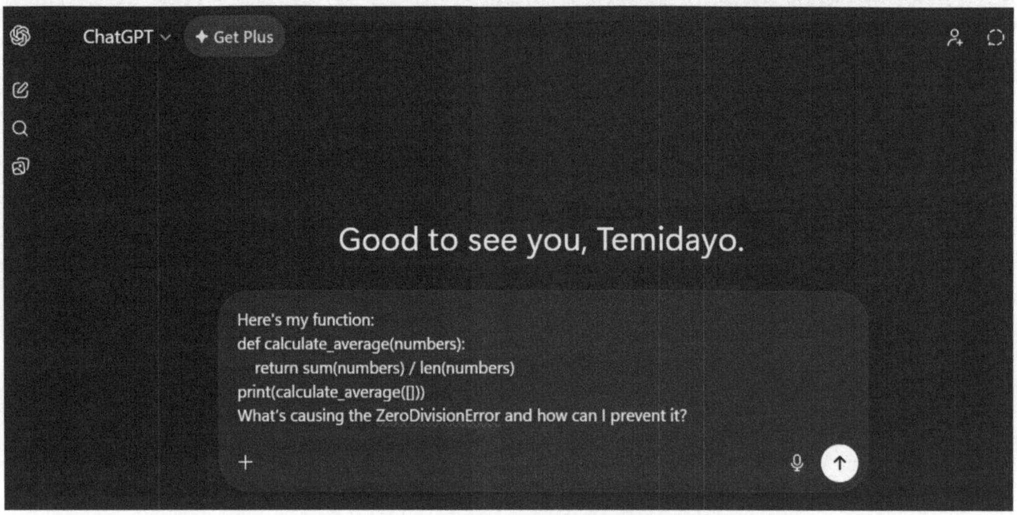

Figure 4.5: *ChatGPT Prompt*

ChatGPT:

The error occurs because you are dividing by the length of an empty list (`0`). You can handle this gracefully:

```
def calculate_average(numbers):
if not numbers:
raise ValueError("Cannot calculate the average of an empty list.")
    return sum(numbers) / len(numbers)
```

This shows how AI can not only fix errors but also teach safe coding patterns, such as adding guard clauses.

Logic Errors: When Everything Runs, but the Results Lie

Logic errors are trickier. The code executes, but the output is wrong. This is where AI truly shines, helping you reason about intent versus behavior.

Example: Wrong Calculation

```
def calculate_discount(price, discount):
    return price * discount  # should subtract, not multiply

print(calculate_discount(100, 0.2))
```

Output:

```
20.0
```

Expected:

```
80.0
```

Prompt:

The function below is supposed to apply a 20% discount to a price, but it gives the wrong output. What is wrong?

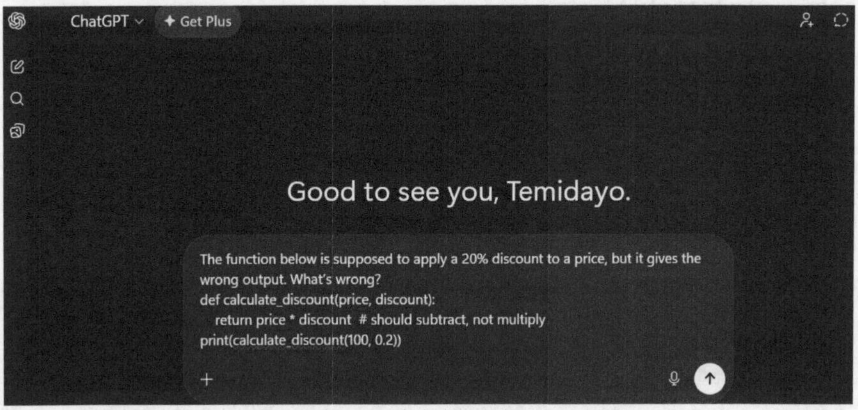

Figure 4.6: ChatGPT Prompt

ChatGPT:

The logic multiplies price and discount instead of subtracting the discount from the price.

Correct version:

```
def calculate_discount(price, discount):
    return price * (1 - discount)
```

This explanation helps the learner *see the intention gap* between what they coded and what they meant, which is a key debugging mindset.

Combining Human Intuition and AI Reasoning

Here is a mini example where AI helps you debug step by step, not just by fixing code, but by reasoning with you.

Scenario: You are building a student grade system.

```
def grade_student(scores):
    average = sum(scores) / len(scores)
    if average > 80:
        return "A"
    elif average > 60:
        return "B"
    elif average > 40:
        return "C"
    else:
        return "D"

print(grade_student([80, 90, 70]))
print(grade_student([]))
```

You get:

```
ZeroDivisionError: division by zero
```

Prompt:

Why am I getting a ZeroDivisionError in this student grading function, and how can I improve the design so it does not crash?

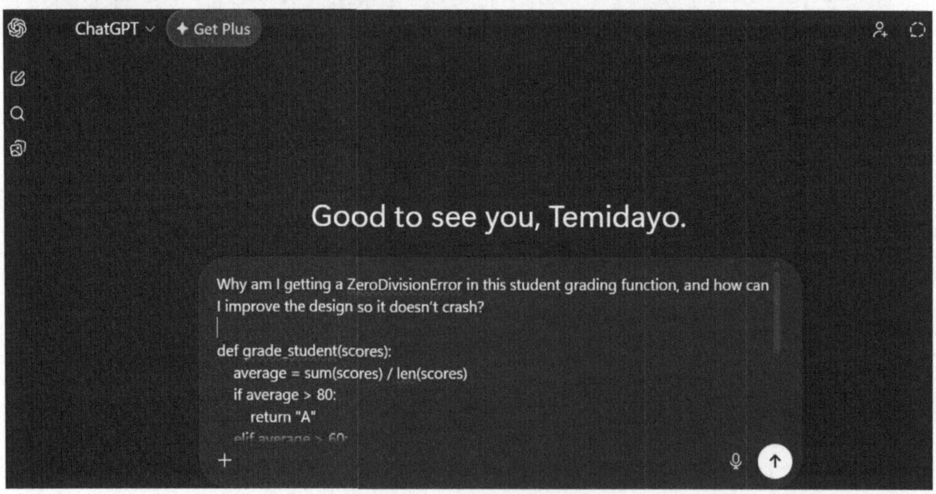

Figure 4.7: ChatGPT Prompt

ChatGPT:

The issue occurs when you pass an empty list. You can add an input validation step. Here is a safer version:

```
def grade_student(scores):
    if not scores:
        return "No scores provided"
    average = sum(scores) / len(scores)
    if average > 80:
        return "A"
    elif average > 60:
        return "B"
    elif average > 40:
        return "C"
    else:
        return "D"
```

You might also consider adding logging or raising a custom error if data is missing.

Step-by-Step Debugging Workflows

Debugging is not a chaotic sprint; it is a disciplined ritual. The better your ritual, the faster you find the problem and the less likely you are to introduce new ones.

The next section provides a repeatable workflow, a set of professional moves you can follow every time something breaks. Let us explore code, terminal commands, and exact prompts you can feed to ChatGPT so you can practice immediately in VS Code.

Before We Begin: Quick Setup Checklist

Run these once in your project folder:

```
# create virtual environment
python -m venv .venv
# activate (mac/linux)
source .venv/bin/activate
# or on Windows
.venv\Scripts\activate
# install test tools (if not already)
pip install pytest pytest-cov
```

Keep a Git branch for experiments:

```
git checkout -b debug/<short-description>
```

Why? You want a safe rollback if a suggested fix explodes.

The Workflow: Six Reproducible Steps

1. **Reproduce and record the failure.**
2. **Narrow the scope (isolate the failing unit).**
3. **Write a failing test.**
4. **Ask ChatGPT with context.**
5. **Apply a candidate fix and run tests.**
6. **Refactor and harden (add tests, logging, guard clauses).**

Let us walk through each step with concrete examples.

Reproduce and Record the Failure

Reproducing the bug reliably is the most underrated step. If it will not fail reliably, you cannot prove a fix.

Example: create `calc.py`

```
# calc.py
def average(values):
    return sum(values) / len(values)
```

Now run an example that triggers a problem:

```
# runner.py
from calc import average
print(average([10, 20, 30]))
print(average([]))   # Oops — will raise ZeroDivisionError
```

Run it:

```
python runner.py
# Traceback... ZeroDivisionError
```

Record the exact command, stack trace, and input that caused it. This will be your reference when you ask ChatGPT and when you write tests.

Narrow the Scope (Isolate the Failing Unit)

Find the smallest code piece that reproduces the error. Here, it is **`average([])`**. Isolation helps you avoid chasing unrelated issues.

Now, create a targeted test file (we will use pytest):

```
# test_calc.py
from calc import average
```

```
import pytest
def test_average_normal():
    assert average([10, 20, 30]) == 20
def test_average_empty():
    assert average([]) == 0  # expected behavior we decide
```

Run the tests:

```
pytest -q
# one test passes, one fails
```

You now have a reproducible failing test—perfect.

Write a Failing Test (Make Expectations Explicit)

This step forces you to decide on the desired behavior. Should `average([])` return 0, None, or raise a custom error? Make that choice before asking for fixes.

Your test above sets the expectation to return `0`. If you prefer raising a descriptive exception, change the test accordingly. This clarity matters when evaluating suggestions.

Ask ChatGPT with Context (the Right Prompt)

Now that the failing test is deliberate, ask ChatGPT. Use the CCS-style prompt: **context, constraints, and goal**.

Example prompt (paste into ChatGPT):

> Context: I have a Python module `calc.py` with `average(values)` that currently does `sum(values)/len(values)`.
>
> Problem: My pytest fails for empty lists (`ZeroDivisionError`).
>
> Constraint: I want the function to return `0` for empty lists (not raise), and keep existing behavior otherwise.
>
> Goal: Provide a small, idiomatic fix and a short explanation (1–2 lines). Also return a version compatible with Python 3.8+.
>
> Code:
>
> ```
> def average(values):
>     return sum(values) / len(values)
> ```

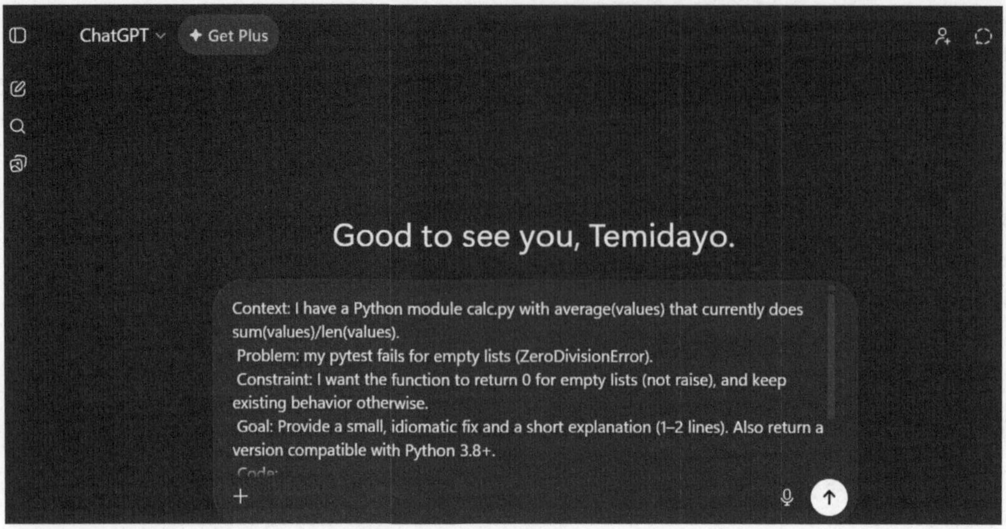

Figure 4.8: *ChatGPT Prompt*

This prompt gives ChatGPT everything it needs. Expect an answer such as:

```
def average(values):
    if not values:
        return 0
    return sum(values) / len(values)
```

ChatGPT will likely explain *why* (guard clause prevents division by zero) and mention edge cases.

Why this prompt works: you gave input, exact desired behavior, and code—no guessing.

Apply Candidate Fix and Run Tests

Update **`calc.py`** and re-run:

```
pytest -q
# all tests pass
```

If tests still fail, iterate: provide the failing trace + updated code + what you tried to ChatGPT.

A useful troubleshooting prompt after a failed attempt:

I applied your suggestion, but pytest still fails with this traceback [paste]. Here is my updated code [paste]. Please identify why tests still fail or propose an alternative fix.

This keeps the conversation focused and constructive.

Refactor and Harden

Once tests pass, do not stop. Take two minutes to harden:

- Add a docstring for `average`.
- Add a test for non-numeric inputs.
- Add a type guard or raise an informative `ValueError`.

Example polished function:

```
def average(values):
    """
    Calculate the average of an iterable of numbers.

    - Returns 0 for empty sequences.
    - Raises TypeError if the input is not iterable.
    - Raises ValueError if any item is non-numeric.
    """
    if not hasattr(values, "__iter__"):
        raise TypeError("Input must be an iterable.")

    total = 0.0
    count = 0

    for value in values:
        try:
            total += float(value)
            count += 1
        except (TypeError, ValueError):
            raise ValueError("All items must be numeric.")

    if count == 0:
        return 0

    return total / count
```

Add tests to cover:

- `average([1, "a"])` raises `ValueError`
- `average([5]) == 5.0`

Run the full test suite again.

A Concrete Debugging Chain for a Subtle Bug

Now, a slightly more involved issue – a performance bug and a wrong result when the dataset has zeros.

Scenario: A function removes outliers by dividing by the mean, but when zeros are present, the result explodes.

Code:

```
# normalize.py
def normalize(values):
    mean = sum(values) / len(values)
    return [v / mean for v in values]
```

Problem: If mean is 0, division fails; if the values are floats close to zero, the results get huge.

Workflow:

1. Reproduce: create **`test_normalize`** with **`normalize([0,0,0])`** expecting **`[0,0,0]`**.
2. Isolate and write a failing test.
3. Prompt ChatGPT:

   Context: `normalize(values)` divides each element by the mean.

   Problem: When the mean is 0 or near-zero, the results are invalid.

   Constraint: The function should return the original list of zeros when mean == 0, and otherwise perform normalization safely.

   Goal: Provide a robust, numeric-safe implementation and explain tradeoffs.

ChatGPT might suggest:

- Check **`if abs(mean) < 1e-12: return values`**.
- Or use a small epsilon to avoid division instability.
- Or normalize using **`statistics.mean`** and fallback.

Suggested code:

```
def normalize(values, eps=1e-12):
    mean = sum(values) / len(values)
    if abs(mean) <= eps:
        return values[:]  # avoid dividing by zero or tiny mean
    return [v / mean for v in values]
```

Add tests for **`eps`** behavior, run **`pytest`**, iterate.

AI-Assisted Code Refactoring: Cleaner Functions, Modularity, and the DRY Principle

Refactoring is the quiet work that turns a prototype into a product. It is the difference between a folder full of useful scripts and a codebase that someone else or your future self can confidently pick up and extend. Refactoring is not cosmetic. It reduces bugs, makes tests meaningful, and lets teams move faster.

I once joined a company where every change required a week of code studying. The reason was not cleverness; it was duplication, implicit side effects, and functions that did six things at once. Refactoring that code into well-named pieces slashed our bug rate and made onboarding a matter of hours, not days. That is why refactoring is not optional; it is professional hygiene.

Tools in Your VS Code Toolbox

Open the terminal in your virtual environment and install:

```
pip install pytest black flake8 mypy
```

- **`pytest`** for tests,
- **`black`** for consistent formatting,
- **`flake8`** for basic linting or detecting common smells, and
- **`mypy`** for optional static typing checks.

These tools help you verify that a refactor preserved behavior and improved clarity.

Before: A Realistic, Messy Function

Save this as **`report.py`** and run this snippet. It works, but it is hard to follow and hard to test.

```
# report.py
import csv
from collections import defaultdict
from datetime import datetime

def generate_report(file_path):
    rows = []
    with open(file_path, newline='') as f:
        reader = csv.reader(f)
        for r in reader:
            rows.append(r)
    totals = defaultdict(float)
    for r in rows:
        date = datetime.strptime(r[0], "%Y-%m-%d")
        region = r[1]
        amount = float(r[2])
        if amount > 0:
            totals[region] += amount
```

```
    avg = {}
    for region, total in totals.items():
        count = sum(1 for r in rows if r[1] == region and float(r[2]) > 0)
        avg[region] = total / count
    report_text = "Report\\n"
    for region, total in totals.items():
        report_text += f"{region}: total={total:.2f},
avg={avg[region]:.2f}\\n"
    return report_text
```

Problems to spot:

- Single function doing IO, parsing, aggregation, and formatting.
- Repetition: converting **`r[2]`** to **`float`** in multiple places.
- Hard-coded indices (**`r[0]`**, **`r[1]`**, **`r[2]`**) obscure meaning.
- Difficult to unit test since IO and logic are mixed.

Identify Refactor Goals

Before changing anything, write a simple test that captures the current behavior so that you can validate your refactor.

Create `test_report.py`:

```
# test_report.py
from report import generate_report
import tempfile

def test_generate_report():
    data = "2025-01-01,North,100\\n2025-01-02,North,50\\n2025-01-
01,South,200\\n"
    with tempfile.NamedTemporaryFile("w+", delete=False) as tf:
        tf.write(data)
        tf.flush()
        output = generate_report(tf.name)
    assert "North: total=150.00" in output
    assert "South: total=200.00" in output
```

Run it:

```
pytest -q
```

If the test passes, you have captured behavior; now refactor with safety.

Refactor goals:

1. Replace magic indices with a small `Row` parser.

2. Separate IO (reading CSV) from aggregation logic.
3. Remove repeated conversions of `r[2]` by normalizing rows once.
4. Add docstrings and type hints.
5. Keep the same output format for compatibility.

Small, Local Refactors (Extract Function)

Make a minimal change first: Extract code that parses a CSV row into a **dict** or **dataclass**.

Update **report.py**:

```
# report.py
import csv
from collections import defaultdict
from dataclasses import dataclass
from datetime import datetime
from typing import Dict, List

@dataclass
class SaleRow:
    date: datetime
    region: str
    amount: float

def parse_row(row: List[str]) -> SaleRow:
    date = datetime.strptime(row[0], "%Y-%m-%d")
    region = row[1]
    amount = float(row[2])
    return SaleRow(date=date, region=region, amount=amount)

def generate_report(file_path: str) -> str:
    rows = []
    with open(file_path, newline='') as f:
        reader = csv.reader(f)
        for r in reader:
            rows.append(parse_row(r))
    totals = defaultdict(float)
    for r in rows:
        if r.amount > 0:
            totals[r.region] += r.amount
    avg = {}
    for region, total in totals.items():
        count = sum(1 for r in rows if r.region == region and r.amount > 0)
```

```
        avg[region] = total / count
    report_text = "Report\\n"
    for region, total in totals.items():
        report_text += f"{region}: total={total:.2f},
avg={avg[region]:.2f}\\n"
    return report_text
```

Re-run tests. They should still pass. You have reduced duplication (converting the amount once) and made parsing explicit.

Ask the Assistant for Focused Refactors

Now, use ChatGPT to help you further refactor. Good prompts are specific and include constraints.

Prompt to paste into ChatGPT (or your preferred assistant):

```
Context: I have a report generator function that reads a CSV, parses rows, aggregates totals, computes averages, and formats a text report. I separated parsing into `parse_row`. The remaining generate_report still mixes IO and aggregation and uses loops to compute averages.

Constraint: Keep the same textual output format (for compatibility with other systems) and preserve current behavior for positive amounts only. Use the Python standard library only.

Goal: Suggest a refactor that separates reading, aggregation, and formatting into three functions: `read_sales(file_path) -> List[SaleRow]`, `aggregate(sales) -> Dict[str, Dict[str,float]]` (return totals and counts), and `format_report(aggregation) -> str`. Return code only.
```

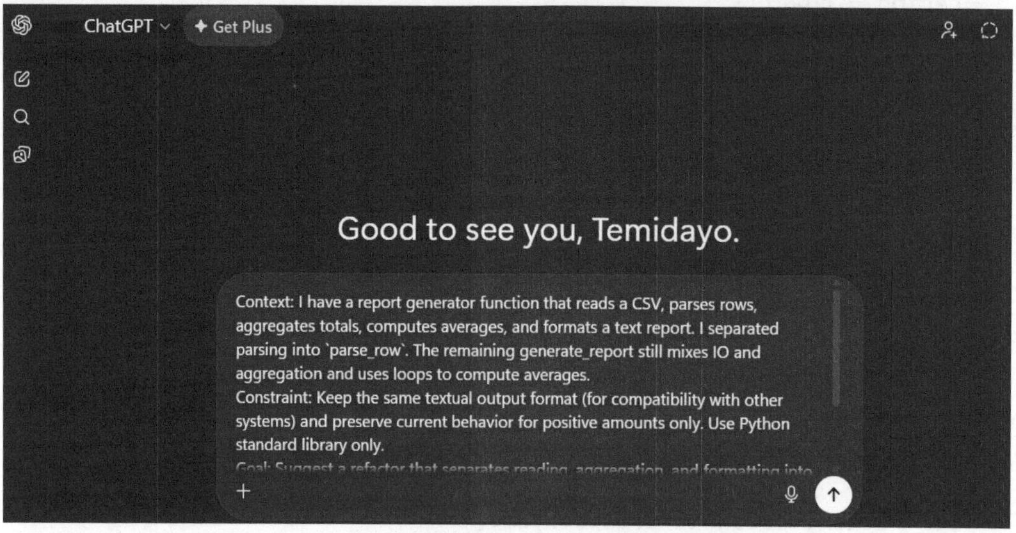

Figure 4.9: *ChatGPT Prompt*

A good assistant response will include the three function definitions and show how to wire them together. Paste the suggested code into your file, run tests, and iterate.

Apply Modularization and the DRY Principle

A well-refactored version (after asking and iterating):

```
# report.py
import csv
from collections import defaultdict
from dataclasses import dataclass
from datetime import datetime
from typing import Dict, Iterable, List, Tuple

@dataclass
class SaleRow:
    date: datetime
    region: str
    amount: float

def parse_row(row: List[str]) -> SaleRow:
    return SaleRow(
        date=datetime.strptime(row[0], "%Y-%m-%d"),
        region=row[1],
        amount=float(row[2])
    )

def read_sales(file_path: str) -> List[SaleRow]:
    sales: List[SaleRow] = []
    with open(file_path, newline='') as f:
        reader = csv.reader(f)
        for r in reader:
            sales.append(parse_row(r))
    return sales

def aggregate(sales: Iterable[SaleRow]) -> Dict[str, Tuple[float, int]]:
    totals: Dict[str, float] = defaultdict(float)
    counts: Dict[str, int] = defaultdict(int)
    for s in sales:
        if s.amount > 0:
            totals[s.region] += s.amount
            counts[s.region] += 1
    return {region: (totals[region], counts[region]) for region in totals}

def format_report(aggregation: Dict[str, Tuple[float, int]]) -> str:
```

```
    lines = ["Report"]
   for region, (total, count) in aggregation.items():
        avg = total / count if count else 0
        lines.append(f"{region}: total={total:.2f}, avg={avg:.2f}")
    return "\n".join(lines) + "\n"

def generate_report(file_path: str) -> str:
    sales = read_sales(file_path)
    aggregation = aggregate(sales)
    return format_report(aggregation)
```

What changed and why it is better:

- **Single Responsibility:** Each function does one thing—easier to test.
- **DRY:** No repeated float conversions; counts and totals are computed together.
- **Modular:** You can reuse `aggregate` with other data sources.
- **Type Hints and Dataclass** make the code self-documenting.

Run tests again—they should still pass.

Testing and Verification after Refactor

Refactoring without tests is faith-based engineering. Your verification checklist:

Run unit tests:

```
pytest -q
```

1. Run formatter and linters:

   ```
     black .
   flake8
   mypy report.py
   ```

2. Fix any warnings that represent real issues (not just style disagreements).
3. Add tests for new modular functions:
   - **`test_read_sales`** using temp files.
   - **`test_aggregate`** feeding constructed `SaleRow` instances.
   - **`test_format_report`** checking formatting exactness.

Example new test:

```
import datetime
from report import SaleRow, aggregate
def test_aggregate_simple():
    sales = [
```

```
        SaleRow(datetime.datetime(2025, 1, 1), "North", 100.0),
        SaleRow(datetime.datetime(2025, 1, 2), "North", 50.0),
        SaleRow(datetime.datetime(2025, 1, 1), "South", 200.0),
    ]
    agg = aggregate(sales)
    assert agg["North"] == (150.0, 2)
    assert agg["South"] == (200.0, 1)
```

Run tests and ensure that they pass.

Evolve without Breaking (Additions and Guardrails)

After a refactor, guardrails stop regressions:

- Add a test for edge cases (empty files, negative amounts, and malformed rows).
- If you accept CSVs from multiple sources, consider a **`safe_parse_row`** that returns `Optional[SaleRow]` and logs a warning for malformed lines.

Add logging instead of prints for production code:

```
import logging
logger = logging.getLogger(__name__)
```

- If performance matters (large files), consider streaming processing using generators rather than loading all sales into memory.

Pitfalls and When Not to Refactor

- **Premature Generalization:** Do not abstract for requirements that do not exist. Keep the KISS principle.
- **Breaking Public API:** If other systems rely on exact function signatures or file formats, preserve backward compatibility, or provide compatibility shims.
- **Over-Typing Early:** While hints help, aggressive static typing without tests can slow progress. Add `mypy` checks gradually.

Practical Prompts You Can Use While Refactoring

Use the assistant to suggest small, safe changes and not entire rewrites. Examples:

- *"Given the code below, extract the CSV reading logic into a `read_sales(file_path)` function that returns `List[SaleRow]`. Preserve current behavior. Show changes only."*
- *"Suggest unit tests for the `aggregate` function above. Include edge cases for empty input and negative amounts."*

- *"I want to change the report output to JSON as an optional argument `format='text'|'json'`. Show a minimal and backward-compatible change."*

Keep prompts tightly scoped; ask for code-only answers when you plan to paste and run the code immediately.

Conclusion

If there is one thing every developer eventually learns, it is this: Debugging is not punishment; it is communication. Every error message, stack trace, and unexpected output is your program trying to tell you something. The better you listen, the faster you improve.

With tools such as ChatGPT, debugging is no longer a lonely war against cryptic red lines. It is now a dialogue between you, your code, and a digital collaborator that helps you see what you might have missed. But make no mistake: AI does not replace the instinct that great developers develop over time.

In this chapter, you have learned to treat errors as breadcrumbs, use AI to translate technical noise into human logic, and refactor code not just to "make it work," but to make it **better**—cleaner, modular, and maintainable. In the next chapter, you will learn how to automate tedious tasks using intelligence.

Points to Remember

- AI can interpret, but you must reason.
- Not all errors are created equal.
- Refactoring is preventive debugging.
- Debugging with AI is a conversation, not a command.
- **Single Responsibility:** Each function does one thing.
- **DRY:** No repeated float conversions; counts and totals computed together.
- **Modular:** You can reuse `aggregate` with other data sources.
- **Type Hints and Dataclass** make the code self-documenting.

Hands-on Exercise

1. Copy the following buggy Python snippet:

```
expenses = [{"amount": 100, "category": "Food"}, {"amount": 50,
"category": "Transport"}]
total = 0
for item in expenses:
```

```
    total += item["amounts"]  # typo here
print(total)
```

2. Run it in VS Code. Observe the error.
3. Ask ChatGPT:

   I got a KeyError: 'amounts'. Explain why this happened and how to fix it.
4. Apply the fix (`"amount"` instead of `"amounts"`) and run again.
5. Repeat with a few modifications—introduce strings in place of numbers, or missing keys—and ask the AI to explain why errors occur and how to handle them gracefully.

Key Terms

- **Stack Trace**: The sequence of function calls that led to an error. Think of it as the trail your program leaves behind when something goes wrong.
- **Logic Error**: A flaw in your reasoning; the code runs but does not produce the right result.
- **Runtime Error**: An issue that occurs while the program is executing, often due to unexpected input or missing resources.
- **Syntax Error**: A rule-breaking mistake in your code structure, such as forgetting a colon or misplacing parentheses.
- **Refactoring**: Rewriting and restructuring code to make it cleaner and more efficient without changing what it does.
- **DRY Principle**: "Do Not Repeat Yourself." A reminder to reuse logic instead of duplicating it across your code.
- **Modularization:** Splitting code into smaller, independent parts (modules or functions) for clarity and maintainability.
- **AI-Assisted Debugging**: The use of tools such as ChatGPT to analyze, explain, and suggest solutions for coding issues.

CHAPTER 5
Automating Tedious Tasks

Introduction

If you spend enough time writing code, you eventually face an uncomfortable truth: most of your day disappears into tiny, repetitive tasks that never make it into performance reviews or sprint summaries. Renaming files. Cleaning messy text. Moving logs. Extracting a few lines from a long document. Sending weekly summary emails. Parsing data someone swore was "already structured."

The modern developer's life is a constant negotiation with boredom.

Yet these little tasks, the chores of programming, quietly drain your energy. They break your focus, interrupt creative flow, and stretch simple work into long afternoons. The good news is that Python was built for exactly this world. And when combined with the right strategy and disciplined prompting, it becomes the closest thing to an extra pair of hands you will ever have.

This chapter is about reclaiming your time.

You will learn how to take everyday work and turn it into background processes that run reliably without supervision. We will begin with the fundamentals of automation and move steadily toward more complex workflows. You will build tools that clean data, organize files, process text, scrape the web, and run jobs on a schedule.

Throughout the chapter, you will lean on two skills you have been strengthening since *Chapter 1, Getting Started with AI-Powered Development*: breaking a problem into proper steps and expressing those steps clearly when collaborating with ChatGPT.

You will see how both skills come together to build small but powerful scripts that slot neatly into your daily workflow. You will also see when Python's standard libraries—os, shutil, datetime, and others—are enough on their own and when a workflow needs something extra.

By the end of this chapter, you will not only be comfortable automating tasks but also be confident enough to design your own workflows from scratch.

Structure

In this chapter, we will cover the following topics:

- Using os, shutil, datetime, and schedule Libraries for Workflow Automation
- Common Automation Tasks (File Management, Text Processing, and Scheduling)
- AI-Driven Web Scraping Examples with Requests and BeautifulSoup

Using os, shutil, datetime, and Schedule Libraries for Workflow Automation

If you think about it, every computer is a giant collection of small, predictable rituals. Files appear. Files disappear. Folders grow large. Logs overflow. Backups get forgotten. Humans are terrible at rituals; we get distracted, overwhelmed, or bored. Python, however, has no pride and no complaints. It will happily perform the same task a thousand times.

And when combined with ChatGPT, you get something even more powerful.

os: Your Entry Point into the Operating System

If Python were a person, **os** would be its hands touching your files, opening doors into directories, checking whether paths exist, and generally navigating the filesystem on your behalf.

Most learners underestimate how much automation becomes possible once they understand a handful of os functions. So, let us peel it apart.

Before automating anything, you must know *exactly* what your script sees.

Try this:

```
from pathlib import Path

# Resolve the user's home directory and target the Downloads folder
target = Path.home() / "Downloads"

# List and print all entries in the folder
for item in target.iterdir():
    print(item.name)
```

Run that.

Now, here is where ChatGPT becomes your partner. After printing the folder contents, take that output and paste it into ChatGPT with a prompt such as:

> *"These are the files in my downloads folder. Help me design a sorting strategy to automate organizing them using the os module."*

ChatGPT will pull patterns from the filenames and suggest categories you might not even have thought of, such as images, invoices, app installers, lecture notes, videos, and so on.

This is the point:

The machine sees the raw data, and ChatGPT helps you think about it.

Essential os tools you will use for automation are:

- **`os.listdir()`** → Examine a folder.
- **`os.path.exists()`** → Check if something is already there.
- **`os.makedirs()`** → Create structured folder hierarchies.
- **`os.remove()`** → Delete a file.
- **`os.rename()`** → Rename files in bulk (incredibly powerful).
- **`os.path.join()`** → Combine paths safely across operating systems.

Hands-on: Bulk-renaming practice

```
import os

folder = "/Users/yourname/Downloads"

for index, file in enumerate(os.listdir(folder), start=1):
    base, ext = os.path.splitext(file)
    new_name = f"file_{index}{ext}"
    os.rename(
        os.path.join(folder, file),
        os.path.join(folder, new_name)
    )
```

This creates predictable filenames, excellent for photo albums, scanned sheets, or files exported from inconsistent tools.

Ask ChatGPT to refine it:

> *"Rewrite this renaming script so that it preserves date-created metadata and only renames .jpg files."*

shutil: When Automation Needs Muscle

If os is the pair of hands, shutil is the forklift, built for lifting, copying, moving, archiving, and mirroring folder structures.

The most powerful functions you will use are:

- `shutil.copyfile()`,
- `shutil.copytree()`,
- `shutil.move()`,
- `shutil.rmtree()`, and
- `shutil.make_archive()`: Creates **.zip** or **.tar.gz** archives automatically.

Let us assume you are working on a Python project. You want daily backups stored neatly with timestamps.

```
from pathlib import Path
import shutil
from datetime import datetime

# Define source directory relative to the user's home folder
source = Path.home() / "my_project"
# Create a timestamped backup folder
timestamp = datetime.now().strftime("%Y-%m-%d_%H-%M")
destination = Path.home() / "Backups" / f"my_project_{timestamp}"
# Copy the entire project directory
shutil.copytree(source, destination)
print("Backup completed successfully.")
```

That single script represents hours of repetitive manual labor saved across months.

But do not stop there. ChatGPT can make things even better.

After running this once, tell ChatGPT:

> *"Extend this backup script so it automatically deletes backups older than 10 days and compresses yesterday's backup into a zip file."*

ChatGPT will produce a refined, production-quality version, often with safety checks you did not think of.

datetime: Teaching Your Automations to Understand Time

If you ever want your automation to behave differently today than yesterday or treat weekends differently from weekdays, you need datetime.

Its importance in automation:

- Create unique filenames (**`backup_2025-11-25.zip`**),
- Calculate the age of files,
- Schedule events conditionally ("run only on weekdays"), and
- Add date-based logs without manual writing.

Hands-on: Automatic Daily Log Creation

```
import datetime

today = datetime.date.today()
filename = f"system_log_{today}.txt"

with open(filename, "a") as log:
    log.write(f"{datetime.datetime.now()} - Daily check completed.\n")
```

Logs are the heartbeat of automation. This gives you a steady pulse every time your script runs.

To further improve the quality of this script, you can ask ChatGPT:

> *"Can you help me convert this timestamped log into a rotating log that archives weekly and deletes logs older than 90 days?"*

`schedule`: Teaching Your Script to Run Itself

Automations that require manual execution are not truly automations. The **`schedule`** library lets your Python scripts run on their own.

What schedule is good for:

- Morning reports,
- Hourly cleanups,
- Weekend-only tasks,
- Every 5-minute status check, and
- Business-hour-only routines.

Example: Run a Cleanup Every Night at 11 PM

```
import schedule
import time
import os

def clean_temp():
    folder = "/Users/yourname/Downloads"
```

```
    for f in os.listdir(folder):
        if f.endswith(".tmp"):
            os.remove(os.path.join(folder, f))
            print("Removed:", f)

schedule.every().day.at("23:00").do(clean_temp)

while True:
    schedule.run_pending()
    time.sleep(1)
```

This creates a helper who tidies up daily without complaint.

Let us use ChatGPT to enhance and adapt this scheduler.

Prompt:

> *"Modify this schedule script so it sends me a Telegram message whenever it cleans files, and skips Sundays."*

Combining All Four Libraries: A Real Automation Workflow

Let us now build an integrated workflow to demonstrate the synergy of these tools.

Scenario: Morning Folder Audit

Every day at 8 AM:

1. Scan your downloads folder,
2. Sort files into categories,
3. Create a timestamped backup,
4. Log everything in daily logs,
5. Delete temporary junk, and
6. Notify you when done.

The following is a simplified backbone you can extend:

```
from pathlib import Path
import shutil
from datetime import datetime
import schedule
import time

# Define user-agnostic paths
```

```
DOWNLOADS = Path.home() / "Downloads"
BACKUP_ROOT = Path.home() / "Backups"

def morning_audit():
    now = datetime.now()

    # 1. Categorize files safely
    for item in DOWNLOADS.iterdir():
        if not item.is_file():
            continue  # Skip folders

        # Safely extract file extension
        _, ext = item.stem, item.suffix.lower()
        category = "others"

        if ext in [".jpg", ".png"]:
            category = "images"
        elif ext in [".pdf", ".docx"]:
            category = "documents"
        elif ext in [".mp4", ".mov"]:
            category = "videos"

        dest_dir = DOWNLOADS / category
        dest_dir.mkdir(exist_ok=True)

        shutil.move(str(item), dest_dir / item.name)

    # 2. Backup downloads folder
    backup_name = f"backup_{now:%Y%m%d_%H%M}"
    backup_path = BACKUP_ROOT / backup_name
    shutil.copytree(DOWNLOADS, backup_path)

    # 3. Log activity
    log_file = Path.cwd() / f"log_{now:%Y-%m-%d}.txt"
    with log_file.open("a") as log:
        log.write(f"{now}: Audit completed.\n")

    print("Morning audit done.")

# Schedule the task
schedule.every().day.at("08:00").do(morning_audit)

while True:
    schedule.run_pending()
    time.sleep(1)
```

Now, take this script to ChatGPT and say:

> *"Improve this workflow so that it compresses old backups, sends a report email, and excludes files larger than 1GB."*

Common Automation Tasks

Automation does not begin with complicated systems. It often begins with the things we do so frequently that we barely notice them anymore. Your downloads folder slowly turns into a landfill. You rename screenshots one by one. You hunt inside large text files for one tiny line. You run the same morning checks every single day.

This is about showing you how to turn these low-level chores into tidy, predictable, hands-off processes with Python as your tool and ChatGPT as your thinking partner.

Do not wait until you "understand everything". The fastest way to learn automation is by automating something *today*.

File Management Automation

Most people treat their computer like a storage container. Programmers treat it like a system. That shift begins with learning how to command files and folders, not just click through them.

Python's os and shutil libraries give you superpowers:

- creating folders,
- deleting temporary files,
- renaming files in bulk,
- sorting files by type, size, or date, and
- backing up entire directories.

With ChatGPT helping you structure the logic, you stop guessing and start working with intention.

Sorting Files into Folders by File Type

Create a folder called **`demo_files`** and drop random files inside: PDFs, JPGs, MP4s, DOCXs.

Then give ChatGPT this structured prompt:

> *"I have a folder called demo_files with mixed file types.*
>
> *Generate a Python script I can run in VS Code that sorts all files into subfolders based on their extension.*

List any libraries I must install.

Use os *and* shutil *only*."

ChatGPT should give you something like:

```
from pathlib import Path
import shutil

source = Path("demo_files")

for item in source.iterdir():
    if item.is_file():
        # Safely extract file extension
        ext = item.suffix.lower() or "no_extension"

        target_dir = source / ext.lstrip(".")
        target_dir.mkdir(exist_ok=True)

        shutil.move(str(item), target_dir / item.name)

print("Sorting completed.")
```

Run it.

Watch what happens.

Then modify the script:

- Add logging.
- Move only files larger than 2MB.
- Exclude .txt files.

Whenever you feel stuck, ask ChatGPT:

"*Help me adjust the script so it only moves files above* 2MB."

Bulk File Renaming

Renaming 200 screenshots manually is torture.

But with a 10-line script, it becomes trivial.

Put 20 files into **`rename_test/`**.

Then give ChatGPT:

"*Write a Python script I can run in VS Code that renames all files in the folder* *`rename_test`*, *using the pattern:*

`image_001.ext`, *`image_002.ext`*, *and so on.*

Also, explain how to preserve original extensions."

You will get code similar to:

```
import os

folder = "rename_test"
files = os.listdir(folder)

for index, filename in enumerate(files, start=1):
    ext = filename.split(".")[-1]
    new_name = f"image_{index:03d}.{ext}"
    os.rename(
        os.path.join(folder, filename),
        os.path.join(folder, new_name)
    )

print("Renaming completed.")
```

Modify it so that renamed files include a timestamp:

`image_001_20251125.jpg`

Ask ChatGPT:

> *"Append today's date to each filename in* YYYYMMDD *format."*

Cleaning up Large Folders Automatically

Let us handle a scenario that everyone secretly struggles with: the downloads folder.

You can build an automation script that:

- deletes files older than 30 days,
- groups large files into a separate folder, and
- removes **`.zip`** files automatically.

Use this prompt:

> *"Help me write a Python script for* VS Code *that deletes all files in a folder older than 30 days and logs what was deleted.*
>
> *Use* `os`*,* `time`*, and* `datetime` *only."*

Run the script, then try extending it:

- Keep a backup before deleting.
- Move old files instead of deleting.
- Process multiple folders.

Let ChatGPT walk you through each change.

Text Processing Automation

Text processing is one of the most practical automation skills. Whether you work with customer feedback, server logs, emails, transcripts, or random notes, Python can clean, extract, filter, and restructure text in seconds.

Python's text tools:

- **`open()`**: read/write files,
- **`re`**: pattern matching,
- **`.split(), .replace()`**: quick cleanup,
- **`json:`** structured data, and
- **`csv:`** spreadsheets.

Combined with ChatGPT, this becomes a smooth workflow.

Extracting Patterns from Large Text Files

Examples:

- Emails,
- Phone numbers,
- Error codes,
- Timestamps, and
- Specific keywords.

Create a file called logs.txt with mixed content.

Then try this prompt:

> "*Generate a Python script for* VS Code *that extracts all email addresses from* logs.txt *and writes them into* emails.csv.
>
> *Use only the standard library.*"

Expected structure:

```
import re
import csv

with open("logs.txt", "r") as f:
    text = f.read()

pattern = r"[a-zA-Z0-9._%+-]+@[a-zA-Z0-9.-]+\.[a-zA-Z]{2,}"
emails = re.findall(pattern, text)

with open("emails.csv", "w", newline="") as f:
```

```
    writer = csv.writer(f)
    for e in emails:
        writer.writerow([e])

print("Extraction done.")
```

Ask ChatGPT to modify the script to:

- remove duplicates,
- sort results alphabetically, and
- count the number of extracted emails.

Bulk Text Cleanup

ChatGPT can help you build cleanup pipelines, not single scripts, but systems.

Prompt:

> "*Help me clean a text file by removing* HTML *tags, converting to lowercase, and collapsing multiple spaces. Generate a script for* VS Code."

You will get a baseline script.

Then extend it:

- remove numbers,
- keep only alphabetic characters,
- strip stopwords, and
- summarize output.

Each of these tweaks teaches you something new about text automation.

Scheduling Automations

Automation becomes powerful when it runs without you. That is where scheduling comes in.

There are three main approaches:

1. Manual scheduling: you run scripts yourself,
2. Python scheduling using the schedule library, and
3. OS-level scheduling (cron for macOS/Linux, Task Scheduler for Windows).

For learners, option 2 is the easiest.

Running a Task Every Day

Install the library:

```
pip install schedule
```

Create a script that prints a report every day at 8:00 AM.

Ask ChatGPT:

> "*Write a Python script using the* **`schedule`** *library that runs a function daily at 08:00. Use a while loop to keep the script running.*"

Typical output:

```
import schedule
import time

def daily_task():
    print("Running daily report...")

schedule.every().day.at("08:00").do(daily_task)

while True:
    schedule.run_pending()
    time.sleep(1)
```

Adapt this to:

- clean your downloads folder every Friday,
- backup a directory nightly, and
- send yourself a summary email (you will cover this later in the chapter).

AI-Driven Web Scraping: Practical Examples Using `requests` and `BeautifulSoup`

There is a moment in every developer's journey when the internet stops being a place you browse and becomes a place you **harvest**. Suddenly, you are no longer clicking pages manually; your script is quietly slipping through websites, picking out the exact information you need.

That moment is called *web scraping*.

The Tools You Will Be Using (and Why They Matter)

Web scraping is powered by two foundational Python packages:

`requests`

This is your browser-in-code. It fetches the page's HTML and brings it into your Python environment.

`BeautifulSoup`

This is your scalpel. It lets you slice the HTML into pieces—titles, prices, links, and dates… whatever your automation needs.

To install them:

```
pip install requests beautifulsoup4
```

You should always install explicitly; never assume packages already exist.

Before writing any script in this section, perform these initial steps in VS Code:

1. Create a new folder for scraping exercises.
2. Open VS Code in that folder.
3. Create a new file named **`scrape_demo.py`**.
4. Install required libraries in the terminal (inside VS Code).

Designing an Effective Prompt for ChatGPT

Before we write *any* scraping script, you must craft a clear prompt so ChatGPT knows:

- what you want to scrape,
- from which website,
- what structure the output should have,
- what format the code should return,
- what libraries you will use, and
- any constraints (for example, no external libraries).

A great scraping prompt looks like this:

Model Prompt to Send to ChatGPT

```
**"Write a Python script using requests and BeautifulSoup to scrape the
following website:
 [insert URL]
```

I want to extract these items:

- [item 1],
- [item 2], and
- [item 3].

Return the results as a list of dictionaries.
The script must:

- include explanatory comments,
- handle missing fields gracefully,
- use try/except blocks,
- avoid external dependencies,
- work in VS Code, and
- assume the user will run pip install requests beautifulsoup4.

Generate clean, readable code only, no extra text."**

You will notice the prompt is compact but comprehensive. ChatGPT knows exactly what to produce.

You are providing constraints that force clarity.

This is the CCG framework in action: **Context → Constraints → Goal.**

Now, let us walk through three practical scraping scenarios that you can build and run immediately.

Practical Example 1: Scraping Blog Article Titles

Let us assume you want to scrape the titles of the latest blog posts from a simple website.

Here is exactly what the learner should type into ChatGPT:

Efficient Prompt

**"Generate a Python script that uses requests and BeautifulSoup to scrape the latest blog post titles from https://blog.python.org.

Extract:

- title text
- link to the article

Return the output as a list of dictionaries.
Include comments to explain each section of the script."**

The following is a trimmed-down example of the kind of code a learner will receive:

```
import requests
from bs4 import BeautifulSoup
import time

url = "https://blog.python.org"
response = requests.get(url)
time.sleep(1)  # Polite pause

soup = BeautifulSoup(response.text, "html.parser")

posts = []
items = soup.select(".post-title a")

for item in items:
    posts.append({
        "title": item.get_text(strip=True),
        "link": item["href"]
    })

print(posts)
```

You can run this in VS Code and see the scraped titles appear instantly.

The "wow" moment happens here.

Practical Example 2: Scraping Product Prices from an E-commerce Page

We now raise the stakes: we are scraping structured data—names, prices, and ratings.

Let us craft the correct ChatGPT prompt.

Efficient Prompt

```
**"Write a Python script using requests and BeautifulSoup to scrape
product information from this sample page:
 https://books.toscrape.com/

Extract:

    •  book title
    •  price
    •  availability status

Return the results in a JSON-like list of dicts.
 Include error handling for missing fields."**
```

Expected Code Response

```
import requests
from bs4 import BeautifulSoup
import time

url = "https://books.toscrape.com/"
response = requests.get(url)
time.sleep(1)  # Polite pause

soup = BeautifulSoup(response.text, "html.parser")

books = []

for product in soup.select(".product_pod"):
    books.append({
        "title": product.h3.a["title"],
        "price": product.select_one(".price_color").get_
text(strip=True),
        "availability": product.select_one(".instock.availability").
get_text(strip=True),
    })

print(books)
```

I encourage you to take the result and ask ChatGPT further:

> *"Convert this into a CSV exporter."*

ChatGPT will extend the script elegantly.

Practical Example 3: Scraping Paginated Data (Full Workflow)

Now, we introduce a real-world case—pagination. Most developers often struggle with it, so let us make ChatGPT do the heavy lifting.

Efficient Prompt

`**"Write a Python script using requests and BeautifulSoup to scrape all pages from https://quotes.toscrape.com/.`

`Extract:`

- `quote text,`
- `author name, and`
- `tags.`

The script must:

- follow pagination links until no more pages exist,
- store results in a list of dictionaries,
- contain explanatory comments, and
- require no external libraries beyond requests and BeautifulSoup."**

ChatGPT Will Produce Something Like This

```
import requests
from bs4 import BeautifulSoup
import time
base_url = "https://quotes.toscrape.com"
page_url = "/page/1/"
quotes = []

while page_url:
    response = requests.get(base_url + page_url)
    soup = BeautifulSoup(response.text, "html.parser")

    for q in soup.select(".quote"):
        quotes.append({
            "text": q.select_one(".text").get_text(strip=True),
            "author": q.select_one(".author").get_text(strip=True),
           "tags": [tag.get_text(strip=True) for tag in q.select(".tag")],
        })
    next_link = soup.select_one("li.next a")
    page_url = next_link["href"] if next_link else None

    time.sleep(1)  # Critical: throttle between pages
print(quotes)
```

Conclusion

By this point, you have seen how automation shifts from something abstract to something you can actually hold in your hands: a script that sorts files you do not want to deal with, cleans text you do not have the patience for, schedules tasks your memory cannot carry, and scrapes the web like a quiet assistant who never needs a break.

The goal of this chapter was not to overwhelm you with tools. It was to help you build a new habit:

Whenever you find yourself repeating a task, your first instinct should be: "*Can Python and ChatGPT take this off my plate?*"

You have learned how the standard libraries—**`os`**, **`shutil`**, **`datetime`**, **and `schedule`**—pull real weight in practical workflows and how ChatGPT becomes your technical partner in turning intentions into working pipelines. You have also stepped into the world of web scraping. where the internet becomes a structured source of data instead of a place you manually browse.

In the next chapter, we will explore how to leverage AI to build a working Python game.

Points to Remember

- **Automation thrives on clarity.** Before writing code, define exactly what needs to happen, inputs, outputs, and rules.
- **Start small, chain later.** Break automations into small scripts before combining them into larger workflows.
- **ChatGPT boosts your reasoning.** Use it for structure, explanations, and improvements, but still understand what the script does.
- **Standard libraries cover most real-world tasks.** **`os`**, **`shutil`**, **`datetime`**, and **`schedule`** can automate half of what professionals do daily.
- **Web scraping is pattern recognition.** Once you understand how to target the right HTML elements, the rest is simply iteration.
- **Your automation scripts should be reusable.** Clean functions, predictable structure, and clear comments make your scripts future-proof.

Key Terms

- **Automation:** Using code to execute repetitive tasks without manual effort.
- **Workflow:** A series of automated steps that run in sequence to achieve a goal.
- **Standard Library:** Built-in Python modules that require no external installation.
- **Selector:** A pattern (CSS-like) used to locate elements in an HTML page during scraping.
- **Scheduler:** A function or library that triggers tasks at set times or intervals.
- **Idempotent Script:** A script that can run multiple times without causing unintended changes.

Your Challenge: Build a Complete "Morning Automation" Script

Create a Python automation workflow that does the following every morning at 8:00 AM:

1. Scrapes today's top headlines from a public news website (for example, *BBC, Reuters, or a local site*).
2. Saves the headlines into a timestamped text file inside a folder named **`daily_news/`**.
3. Moves yesterday's file into an **`archive/`** folder automatically.
4. Cleans the text by removing extra whitespace or line breaks.
5. Schedules the entire task with the **`schedule`** library.

Rules

- You must generate your code in collaboration with ChatGPT using the CCG framework.
- You must use only:

  `requests`, **`BeautifulSoup`**, **`os`**, **`shutil`**, **`datetime`**, and **`schedule`**.
- All file paths must be relative, not absolute.
- The script should run in VS Code without modifications.

CHAPTER 6
Making an Interactive Game

Introduction

There is something powerful about building a game. It turns abstract programming ideas into something you can touch—buttons you press, choices you make, characters that react, and outcomes that change depending on your decisions.

Games are where logic becomes meaningful.

Most people meet programming for the first time through exercises—printing messages, looping over numbers, and calculating things nobody asked for. Games flip that story. They give you a world to control. They give you a problem that responds to your imagination.

In this chapter, you are designing an experience.

You will decide how players move, what rules they obey, what obstacles they face, and what rewards they get.

Throughout the chapter, you will use ChatGPT the same way many professional developers do today. You will brainstorm game ideas, explore mechanics, refine logic, and debug behavior through conversation. Rather than memorizing syntax in isolation, you will learn how loops, conditionals, functions, and input handling work together inside a real system.

Structure

In this chapter, we will cover the following topics:

- Introduction to Game Development Basics in Python
- Using AI to Brainstorm Game Ideas and Mechanics
- Structuring Game Logic with Loops, Conditionals, and Functions

- Interactive Input Handling with Python
- Adding Visuals and Interactivity with pygame

Introduction to Game Development Basics in Python

Game development looks complex when you observe it from the outside: moving objects, scores updating, visuals repainting in real time, and characters responding instantly to your actions. But underneath all that, every game, no matter how beautiful or chaotic, runs on a small collection of core ideas.

Python gives you simple entry points into these ideas. You do not need to be a graphics engineer or a math genius. You only need to understand **loops, conditions, state, and input and** how they work together to create the illusion of a living world.

The Game Loop

Every interactive game, whether it is a text adventure or a fast-paced racing game, runs on a loop.

This loop repeats forever until the player quits.

Inside this loop, the game:

1. Listens for player actions,
2. Updates its state based on those actions,
3. Redraws the scene or prints the next message,
4. Waits briefly, and
5. Repeats.

If you strip a game to its skeleton, it looks like this:

```
running = True

while running:
    handle_input()
    update_game_state()
    render_screen()
```

This is the *rhythm* of your game.

Everything else is decoration.

When you ask ChatGPT to help you build a game, it is a good idea to start with:

- A loop,

- Some variable that represents the current state, and
- A basic structure for handling input.

This gives the assistant something concrete to build on.

The Memory of Your Game

Games are not static. Something is always changing:

- A player's position,
- A score,
- A countdown timer,
- Health,
- Enemy behavior, and
- Inventory items.

These pieces of information make up the **state**.

Without a state, a game cannot evolve.

With too much state and no structure, it becomes chaos.

Here is a beginner-friendly state example:

```
player = {
    "x": 5,
    "y": 5,
    "health": 3,
    "score": 0
}
```

Now, your player exists in the world as something you can modify inside the game loop.

One useful way to bring ChatGPT into this step is to ask it to:

- Suggest what state a game idea should track.
- Show you how to structure that state cleanly.
- Propose a better data structure if your code starts getting messy.

The Player's Voice

Games are conversations.

The player acts, the world reacts.

In Python, this can start simply:

```
move = input("Your move (left/right/up/down): ")
```

But as your game gets more advanced—especially when you start using libraries such as `Pygame`, input becomes event-based. That means you do not "stop and ask." You *listen* continuously.

ChatGPT can help translate your plain idea ("I want pressing W to move the character up") into the correct code structure for handling events.

Ask for things such as:

- "Show me how to detect key presses inside a loop."
- "How do I prevent movement from being too fast?"
- "How do I map keys to actions without writing messy `if` chains?"

These prompts give you code plus explanations, exactly what you need when learning game input systems.

Decision-Making inside the Game

Without conditions, everything in a game would behave the same way forever. Conditions introduce **choice** and **consequence**.

Example:

```
if enemy_health <= 0:
    print("Enemy defeated!")
```

Or movement boundaries:

```
if player["x"] < 0:
    player["x"] = 0
```

Or game-ending scenarios:

```
if player["health"] <= 0:
    running = False
    print("Game over!")
```

Every decision your game makes comes from simple conditions. And whenever your logic starts to grow complicated, you can ask ChatGPT to:

- Break it into smaller functions.
- Rewrite the conditions so that they are clearer.
- Propose safer boundary checks.
- Explain unexpected behavior.

A Basic Text-Based Game Skeleton

Here is a starter template you might generate through ChatGPT:

```
running = True
player_pos = 0

while running:
    print(f"Your position: {player_pos}")
    move = input("Move left (L), right (R), or quit (Q): ").lower()

    if move == "l":
        player_pos -= 1
    elif move == "r":
        player_pos += 1
    elif move == "q":
        running = False
        print("You quit the game.")
    else:
        print("Invalid input!")

    if player_pos == 10:
        print("You reached the goal! You win!")
        running = False
```

This tiny little world already shows:

- the game loop,
- interaction,
- state updates,
- conditions, and
- a win scenario.

Using AI to Brainstorm Game Ideas and Mechanics

One of the most exciting parts of game development is coming up with the idea itself. But ideas can be messy, vague, or overwhelming. You might have a vision in your head – "I want a maze game with traps"—but turning that mental image into actionable steps for Python can feel daunting.

This is where collaboration with ChatGPT becomes invaluable. It helps you **refine ideas, explore possibilities, and structure mechanics** in ways that are ready to code.

Turning Concepts into Game Mechanics

Every game starts with a concept: a challenge, a goal, or an interaction. But concepts need rules.

For example:

- **Concept**: A character navigates a dungeon to collect treasures.
- Mechanics derived from the concept:
    - Movement in four directions,
    - Randomly placed obstacles,
    - Score counter for collected treasures, and
    - Health system for traps.

When you feed your ideas to ChatGPT, focus on describing the goal and constraints rather than the code itself:

> *"I want a 2D maze game where the player collects coins, avoids traps, and wins when reaching the exit. Suggest a list of mechanics and functions I will need in Python."*

From this prompt, ChatGPT can output a structured list of:

- Game loop steps,
- Variables and state to track,
- Conditional checks for player actions, and
- Functions to update scores, health, or position.

This gives you a blueprint before you write any code.

Brainstorming Variations

One of the hidden strengths of this process is exploring variations quickly. You can ask for multiple ways to implement a mechanic:

> *"Show three different ways to handle trap damage in a Python game. Include pros and cons for each."*

Now, instead of spending hours debating design choices alone, you get concrete options to consider. You can even ask ChatGPT to explain why one approach might be better for performance or readability.

Structuring Game Functions

Once the mechanics are defined, you can start structuring functions. For instance, using the earlier maze example:

- `move_player()` → handles movement and boundaries
- `check_collision()` → checks for traps, walls, or coins
- `update_score()` → increases score when a coin is collected
- `render_state()` → prints or draws the current game board

ChatGPT can propose function signatures, suggest parameters, or even provide simple starter code. For example:

```
def move_player(position, direction, maze):
    # Update position based on direction
    # Ensure player stays within maze bounds
    return new_position
```

Encouraging Creativity and Iteration

Brainstorming with ChatGPT is not just about generating functions. It is about exploring creative twists:

- Power-ups or bonuses,
- Randomized enemy movement,
- Variable difficulty, and
- Mini-games within the main game.

You can ask the assistant to suggest fun variations:

> *"Give five unique power-ups for a maze game that could change gameplay dynamics."*

This keeps your project exciting and teaches you to think like a game designer, not just a coder.

From Idea to Actionable Steps

The final goal of brainstorming is to have a concrete list of mechanics and functions you can implement. A good workflow looks like this:

1. Describe your game concept in a few sentences.
2. Ask ChatGPT to list mechanics and required functions.
3. Review the suggestions, refine what makes sense.
4. Ask for starter code snippets or function templates.
5. Begin coding while iterating on the mechanics with the assistant.

Always treat ChatGPT's suggestions critically. Ask for multiple options, check logic, and ensure the design aligns with your vision. Think of it as a partner who helps you *explore possibilities quickly*, but you remain in control of the creative direction.

Structuring Game Logic with Loops, Conditionals, and Functions

Now that you have a clear list of mechanics and ideas for your game, it is time to turn those concepts into working Python code. This is where structure matters: how your code flows, how decisions are made, and how repeated actions are handled. A well-structured game is not just easier to build; it is easier to debug, extend, and optimize.

The Game Loop

At the heart of every interactive game is a loop that repeats continuously, processing input, updating state, and rendering outputs. It is the rhythm of your game.

For example:

```
running = True

while running:
    user_input = input("Move (L/R/U/D) or Q to quit: ").lower()
    update_player_position(user_input)
    check_collisions()
    render_game_state()
```

Here is what each part does:

- **User input:** Captures the player's actions.
- **State update:** Moves the player or updates other game variables.\
- **Collision check:** Determines if the player hits a wall, enemy, or collects an item.
- **Render state:** Displays the current game board, score, or health.

ChatGPT can suggest refinements, for example, adding boundaries or preventing invalid moves, making your loop more robust without you having to guess every edge case.

Using Conditionals to Control Flow

Conditionals allow your game to react intelligently to player actions and game events. Without them, every move would behave the same.

Example:

```
if user_input == "l":
    player_pos -= 1
elif user_input == "r":
```

```
    player_pos += 1
elif user_input == "q":
    running = False
    print("Thanks for playing!")
else:
    print("Invalid move.")
```

Here, each branch ensures a specific response. Conditionals are also useful for:

- Determining win/lose conditions,
- Handling collisions with objects or enemies, and
- Triggering events, such as power-ups or traps.\

ChatGPT can help suggest cleaner conditional logic when things start to get complicated, or propose alternative ways to handle multiple scenarios without messy nested statements.

Organizing Repeated Behavior

Functions let you encapsulate behavior so you do not repeat code. This is crucial in games where multiple actions follow the same pattern.

Example:

```
def move_player(position, direction):
    if direction == "l":
        position -= 1
    elif direction == "r":
        position += 1
    return position
```

By moving movement logic into a function:

- The main loop stays concise.
- Updates or fixes only need to be made once.
- Your code becomes readable and maintainable.

ChatGPT can generate starter functions, suggest parameter names, or even propose alternative logic to make the game mechanics more flexible.

Combining Loops, Conditions, and Functions

The real power comes when you combine these three elements. Here is a small example skeleton:

```
def move_player(pos, move):
```

```
    if move == "l":
        pos -= 1
    elif move == "r":
        pos += 1
    return pos

def check_goal(pos):
    if pos == 10:
        return True
    return False

running = True
player_pos = 0

while running:
    print(f"Position: {player_pos}")
    move = input("Move (L/R) or Q to quit: ").lower()

    if move == "q":
        running = False
        print("Game exited.")
        continue

    player_pos = move_player(player_pos, move)

    if check_goal(player_pos):
        print("You reached the goal!")
        running = False
```

Notice how:

- The loop repeats gameplay steps.
- Conditionals control responses.
- Functions encapsulate repeated logic.

With ChatGPT, you can ask for enhancements, such as:

- Adding obstacles or enemies,
- Keeping track of the score, and
- Adding multiple levels.

All of these build naturally from this structured foundation.

Interactive Input Handling with Python

Games live and breathe on interaction. Every move, every decision, every surprise in your game begins with one simple idea: The player does something, and your program reacts deliberately. Input handling is where your game stops being a script and becomes an experience.

Understanding Interaction in Games

Every moment in a game is shaped by the player's choices.

Even the simplest text-based game:

- waits for the player,
- listens carefully,
- reacts with purpose, and
- and loops back with new consequences.

This cycle forms what designers call the interaction loop, and it is the very thing we now refine.

To show the idea clearly, let us start with a simple example.

A Typical Input Pattern in a Text Adventure

```
command = input("What will you do? ").strip().lower()

if command == "explore":
    explore_forest()
elif command == "rest":
    rest_player()
else:
    print("You stand still, unsure of your next move.")
```

Notice the intentionality:

- **.strip()** removes accidental spaces.
- **.lower()** normalizes the input.
- Each branch leads to a deliberate action.

This is the foundation we will build upon.

Interactive Input in a Continuous Game Loop

Let us revisit the loop structure from earlier and now weave interactivity into it more naturally.

```
running = True

while running:
    print("\nYou are standing at a crossroads.")
```

```
    action = input("Move left (L), right (R), rest (REST), or quit (Q):
").lower()

    if action == "l":
        move_left()
    elif action == "r":
        move_right()
    elif action == "rest":
        rest_player()
    elif action == "q":
        running = False
        print("Thanks for playing!")
    else:
        print("That action isn't possible.")
```

This style works well for:

- decision-based adventures,
- turn-based battles,
- puzzle games, and
- even simple movement systems.

However, as the game grows, the number of possible inputs grows too.

This is where ChatGPT becomes useful. You can ask it to restructure this logic into something more organized.

Try a prompt such as:

"Rewrite this input-handling block using a command-action dictionary so I can add new commands easily."

The model will produce a cleaner structure that keeps your game scalable.

Cleaner Input Handling with a Command Map

As your game gains depth, writing long chains of **elif** statements becomes both tedious and error-prone. A command map organizes your input logic into a predictable, expandable structure.

```
def move_left():
    print("You move left along the path.")

def move_right():
    print("You move right and spot something shining.")

def rest():
```

```
    print("You take a moment to breathe.")

commands = {
    "l": move_left,
    "r": move_right,
    "rest": rest
}

running = True

while running:
    choice = input("Choose L, R, REST, or Q: ").lower()

    if choice == "q":
        print("Game over.")
        break

    action = commands.get(choice)
    if action:
        action()
    else:
        print("Unknown command.")
```

This pattern makes your game modular and easy to extend. When you want to add new commands later, such as **'jump'**, **'inspect'**, **'attack'**, and **'defend'**, you simply drop new entries into the dictionary.

This is the kind of structural thinking that game developers rely on, and it is the reason a tool such as ChatGPT can be so helpful. You give it your current game structure, describe what you want to add, and it suggests the cleanest integration.

Moving from Text to Real-Time Interaction: Intro to pygame Input

When you shift from a text-based game to something animated, using **pygame**, input becomes event-driven. This means the game no longer *waits* for input but *listens* for input while the game loop continues running.

A barebones **pygame** input snippet looks like this:

```
import pygame
pygame.init()

screen = pygame.display.set_mode((600, 400))
running = True
player_x = 300
```

```
while running:
    for event in pygame.event.get():
        if event.type == pygame.QUIT:
            running = False

    keys = pygame.key.get_pressed()
    if keys[pygame.K_LEFT]:
        player_x -= 2
    if keys[pygame.K_RIGHT]:
        player_x += 2

    screen.fill((0, 0, 0))
    pygame.draw.rect(screen, (255, 0, 0), (player_x, 200, 40, 40))
    pygame.display.flip()

pygame.quit()
```

Here is what is happening:

- The game loop never stops running,
- Inputs are checked continuously,
- Player movement feels smooth, and
- Movement is independent of text commands.

This marks a shift from "turn-based" thinking to "real-time" thinking. It is a different mental model, but an exciting one.

If you ever get stuck while writing **pygame** input code, send ChatGPT:

"Explain what part of my pygame event loop is preventing movement from working."

Paste your code. Let the assistant highlight missing conditions, misplaced loops, or stuck event handlers.

Adding Visuals and Interactivity with pygame

By now, you have built the skeleton of your game: Loops, decisions, and interactive input.

But it is time to move from imagination to a moving world where players see things happen, not just read them. If Python is the language of your game logic, **pygame** is the brush that lets you paint motion, color, and space.

Before You Begin: Installing pygame

Make sure **pygame** is installed on your machine:

```
pip install pygame
```

If you run into an installation error, do not guess, but paste the error into ChatGPT with a prompt such as:

"*Explain why pygame is not installing and suggest the next steps based on this error message.*"

The assistant will walk you through it.

Understanding the pygame Game Loop

A pygame game loop runs continuously, refreshing the screen and reading inputs on every cycle. It feels different from the text-based loops earlier because everything happens in **real time.**

A minimal template looks like this:

```
import pygame

pygame.init()
screen = pygame.display.set_mode((800, 600))
pygame.display.set_caption("My First Pygame Window")

running = True

while running:
    for event in pygame.event.get():
        if event.type == pygame.QUIT:
            running = False

    screen.fill((30, 30, 30))  # Dark background
    pygame.display.flip()

pygame.quit()
```

Every **pygame** game you build will follow this structure, no matter how complex it becomes:

1. Initialize the engine,
2. Set up the window,
3. Run a continuous loop,
4. Listen for events,
5. Draw things, and

6. Refresh the display.

Once you understand this cycle, **pygame** becomes far less intimidating.

Drawing Your First Shapes

Games start with simple shapes, rectangles for players, circles for enemies, before evolving into sprites and animated characters.

Here is a basic example:

```
pygame.draw.rect(screen, (255, 0, 0), (100, 200, 50, 50))
pygame.draw.circle(screen, (0, 255, 0), (400, 300), 30)
pygame.draw.line(screen, (0, 120, 255), (0, 0), (800, 600), 5)
```

You can ask ChatGPT:

"Generate a few variations of shapes I can draw in pygame to test my rendering."

It will happily propose triangles, arcs, polygon patterns, and so on.

Making Objects Move

Movement is where **pygame** feels alive.

Let us animate a red square sliding across the screen:

```
import pygame
pygame.init()

screen = pygame.display.set_mode((800, 600))
clock = pygame.time.Clock()

x = 50  # Starting position

running = True
while running:
    for event in pygame.event.get():
        if event.type == pygame.QUIT:
            running = False

    x += 3  # Move 3 pixels per frame

    screen.fill((0, 0, 0))
    pygame.draw.rect(screen, (255, 0, 0), (x, 250, 50, 50))
    pygame.display.flip()

    clock.tick(60)  # Limit to 60 FPS

pygame.quit()
```

Key insight: **`clock.tick(60)`** controls the speed of the game. Without it, your object would zip across the screen far too fast.

If something is not moving the way you want, try:

"Here is my pygame movement code. The object jumps instead of moving smoothly. What's causing it?"

You will usually discover an indentation error, a misplaced screen refresh, or a missing clock.

Using Keyboard Input for Live Movement

This is where **pygame** thrives. Instead of waiting for typed commands, **pygame** checks which keys are pressed every frame.

```
keys = pygame.key.get_pressed()

if keys[pygame.K_LEFT]:
    x -= 5
if keys[pygame.K_RIGHT]:
    x += 5
if keys[pygame.K_UP]:
    y -= 5
if keys[pygame.K_DOWN]:
    y += 5
```

Put It All Together:

```
import pygame
pygame.init()

screen = pygame.display.set_mode((800, 600))
clock = pygame.time.Clock()

x, y = 400, 300

running = True
while running:
    for event in pygame.event.get():
        if event.type == pygame.QUIT:
            running = False

    keys = pygame.key.get_pressed()
    if keys[pygame.K_LEFT]:
        x -= 4
    if keys[pygame.K_RIGHT]:
        x += 4
```

```
    if keys[pygame.K_UP]:
        y -= 4
    if keys[pygame.K_DOWN]:
        y += 4

    screen.fill((20, 20, 20))
    pygame.draw.rect(screen, (255, 200, 0), (x, y, 40, 40))
    pygame.display.flip()
    clock.tick(60)

pygame.quit()
```

The moment you run this, you will feel the difference between a game and a program.

Tip: *If your movement "sticks" or is not smooth, ChatGPT can pinpoint why instantly. Just send your full loop.*

Adding Images Instead of Shapes

One of the milestones in beginner game development is the moment you swap out those plain rectangles for real images. It is the point where a project stops looking like an assignment and begins to feel like a game.

The following is a full example of a minimal image-based game loop.

The player can move a character around the screen using the arrow keys, and both the background and player are images, not shapes.

Before running the code, ask ChatGPT for a small helper prompt such as:

Prompt to ChatGPT:

"*Generate two simple game-ready PNG images for a beginner Pygame project:*

1. *A 64×64 player sprite (top-down), and*
2. *An 800×600 background image.*

   Make them simple and cartoony. Provide them as base64 so I can save them locally."

File Structure (Recommended)

```
game/
  main.py
  assets/
      player.png
      background.png
```

main.py

```
import pygame
import sys

pygame.init()
# Screen settings
WIDTH, HEIGHT = 800, 600
screen = pygame.display.set_mode((WIDTH, HEIGHT))
pygame.display.set_caption("Image-Based Game")

clock = pygame.time.Clock()

# -------- LOAD IMAGES -------- #
background = pygame.image.load("assets/background.png")
background = pygame.transform.scale(background, (WIDTH, HEIGHT))

player_img = pygame.image.load("assets/player.png")
player_img = pygame.transform.scale(player_img, (64, 64))

# Player attributes
player_x = WIDTH // 2
player_y = HEIGHT // 2
player_speed = 4

# Control flag for the main loop
running = True

# Main game loop
while running:
    for event in pygame.event.get():
        if event.type == pygame.QUIT:
            running = False  # Clean exit signal

    # Key presses
    keys = pygame.key.get_pressed()
    if keys[pygame.K_LEFT]:
        player_x -= player_speed
    if keys[pygame.K_RIGHT]:
        player_x += player_speed
    if keys[pygame.K_UP]:
        player_y -= player_speed
    if keys[pygame.K_DOWN]:
        player_y += player_speed
```

```
    # Draw background
    screen.blit(background, (0, 0))

    # Draw player
    screen.blit(player_img, (player_x, player_y))

    # Refresh the display
    pygame.display.flip()
    clock.tick(60)
# Cleanup after the loop ends
pygame.quit()
sys.exit()
```

Your First Visual Prototype

Here is a real-world prompt you can use inside ChatGPT:

Prompt:

"Help me generate a pygame starter template with a moving sprite using arrow keys. Include a player class, update method, and a structured game loop."

The assistant will return a cleaner, object-oriented version that you can build upon.

Example result you might get (simplified to match this book's flow):

```
class Player:
    def __init__(self, x, y):
        self.x = x
        self.y = y
        self.speed = 5
        self.sprite = pygame.image.load("player.png")

    def draw(self, surface):
        surface.blit(self.sprite, (self.x, self.y))

    def move(self, keys):
        if keys[pygame.K_LEFT]:
            self.x -= self.speed
        if keys[pygame.K_RIGHT]:
            self.x += self.speed
        if keys[pygame.K_UP]:
            self.y -= self.speed
        if keys[pygame.K_DOWN]:
            self.y += self.speed
```

Conclusion

Game development has a way of turning abstract concepts into something you can feel.

In this chapter, you shaped behavior, interaction, and cause-and-effect. You watched a blank window evolve into a playable space, one step at a time. And you did it with an AI partner that responded to your ideas, helped you test variations, corrected mistakes, and made creativity less intimidating.

If there is one lesson to carry forward, it is that real magic is not in the tools—it is in the rhythm of asking, testing, adjusting, and refining. Games teach that rhythm better than any theoretical exercise ever could.

In the next chapter, we will explore how to create an Authorship Identification Program using Natural Language Processing (NLP).

Points to Remember

- Game loops are the heartbeat of an interactive program. Everything else plugs into that rhythm.
- Player actions come from input handling, and clean input logic organizes the rest of the game's behavior.
- Structure matters: Separating logic into functions keeps games easier to extend and debug.
- Images replace shapes using simple **`blit()`** operations, but image organization is essential as games scale.
- Iteration is normal. No game mechanic works perfectly on the first try; refinement is part of the craft.
- AI is most helpful when you guide it with clear intent: describe what you want and test its suggestions in small steps.

Key Terms

- **Game Loop**: The ongoing cycle that updates the game state and draws the screen each frame.
- **Event Handling**: Capturing user actions (keyboard and mouse) and turning them into in-game behavior.
- **Sprite**: Any image or visual element drawn on the screen during a game.
- **Blitting**: The process of drawing an image onto the Pygame screen.

- **Frame Rate (FPS)**: How many times the game updates per second. Higher FPS means smoother motion.
- **State**: The current condition of your game at any moment: position, score, health, status, and so on.

Challenge to Solve

Create a simple game where:

- A player image can move around the screen.
- Random "collectible" images appear at different positions.
- Each time the player touches a collectible, it disappears, and the score increases.
- The game ends when the player collects 10 items.
- A scoreboard is displayed in the corner.

What You Must Do (with ChatGPT's Help):

1. Ask ChatGPT to generate:
    a. A player sprite,
    b. A small collectible sprite, and
    c. A simple background.
    (Base64 format for easy saving.)
2. Ask ChatGPT to help structure the game loop using functions (movement, spawning, and collision detection).
3. Implement collision detection using bounding box logic.
4. Draw all objects on the screen and update the score in real time.
5. Add a simple "You Win" message when the score reaches 10.

Chapter 7
Creating an Authorship Identification Program

Introduction

There is something strangely intimate about a person's writing. Even when two people try to say the same thing, they never say it the same way. Some lean on long sentences that wander and return home; others speak in short bursts. Some favor rare, decorative words; others trust familiar ones. And without noticing, each writer leaves a trail, patterns, habits, and fingerprints.

This chapter is about teaching a computer to notice those fingerprints.

We are stepping into the world of Natural Language Processing (NLP). We will approach it the way you now approach most technical problems:

Ask the right questions, give the right prompts, and let AI help you both understand and build.

By the end of this chapter, you will have created a small but surprisingly insightful program, one that can look at a piece of text and make an educated guess about who wrote it. More importantly, you will understand the ideas behind it: how text becomes data, how patterns become features, and how those features become a model.

We will start with the foundations: What makes one person's writing different from another's?

Then we will translate those differences into steps a machine can understand, tokenizing text, removing noise, analyzing frequency, and generating the right features.

You will also see how tools like NLTK, spaCy, and scikit-learn fit naturally into an AI-guided workflow.

Structure

In this chapter, we will cover the following topics:

- Introduction to Authorship Identification and Stylometry
- Using AI to Generate Preprocessing Pipelines for Text Data
- Tokenization, Stemming, and Stopword Removal with NLTK and spaCy
- Feature Extraction: Word Frequency, N-Grams, Sentence Length
- Training a Simple Classifier for Authorship Detection (scikit-learn)

Introduction to Authorship Identification and Stylometry

If you have ever read two writers you love, you already know this: people do not just write differently; they write *distinctively*. Somewhere in the way they choose words, shape sentences, and pace their thoughts, their personality leaks through.

That observation is not new. Historians have used writing style to settle disputes about disputed letters. Literary scholars have used it to speculate on anonymous works. Even in cybersecurity, stylometry is used to detect fake accounts and ghostwritten content.

Stylometry is simply the practice of treating writing style as something we can measure.

What makes stylometry exciting today is that it is no longer limited to experts with PhDs. With Python and an AI assistant, you can analyze writing patterns the same way a professional researcher would, tokenizing text, measuring frequency patterns, comparing sentence structures, and training models to decide which author a piece of text most closely resembles.

Stylometry sits at a beautiful intersection:

- It is creative (you are analyzing writing),
- It is technical (you are crunching numbers), and
- It is practical (the techniques you learn apply to almost every NLP task).

How We Will Use AI in This Chapter

You would not be reading long documentation pages or guessing how a library works. You will learn by prompting, asking ChatGPT to generate codes, explain a concept, or help you experiment.

Throughout this chapter, you will see prompts like:

Prompt Example:

> *"Explain stylometry in simple terms and list the text features that vary most between authors."*

or

> *"Generate Python code to compare the word frequency distributions of two text samples."*

or

> *"What are three writing traits that are usually stable for an author, even if the topic changes?"*

Every time you use prompts like these, you will understand the *why* behind each technique, not just the syntax.

When you look closely at text, you start noticing patterns such as:

- **Vocabulary Choices**

  Some writers prefer plain language; others reach for uncommon words.

- **Sentence Length and Rhythm**

  Short. Direct. Punchy.

  Or long, flowing lines with multiple clauses.

- **Punctuation Habits**

  Some love commas; others use dashes or semicolons as their signature moves.

- **Common Phrases and Repeated Structures**

  Some are fond of certain phrases.

- **Word Frequency Distributions**

  Surprisingly consistent across a person's writing.

These measurable elements become your features, the ingredients your model will use to compare different authors.

Using AI to Generate Preprocessing Pipelines for Text Data

Before we can compare writing styles, build features, or train a classifier, we need to do one vital thing: clean the text. Raw text is messy with punctuation, casing, stop words, repeated spaces, numbers, emojis, and newlines.

If you feed unprocessed text into an NLP model, it behaves like a reader distracted by every smudge on the page.

This is why NLP workflows always begin with a preprocessing pipeline. And instead of building everything from scratch, you will use ChatGPT to generate clean, modular codes that you can customize as your project grows.

Why Preprocessing Matters

Two authors might use similar vocabulary but differ in style.

Example:

Author A: "*I really enjoyed the afternoon. Everything felt calm.*"

Author B: "*The afternoon was delightful; a rare moment of calm.*"

If you strip the text carelessly, both sentences could look the same.

Good preprocessing balances cleaning noise with preserving meaningful patterns.

Using ChatGPT to Build Your First Preprocessing Pipeline

Let us start with a simple but complete example. Install the required packages first, so the learner never gets stuck.

Required Installations

Run these in your terminal:

```
pip install nltk
pip install spacy
python -m spacy download en_core_web_sm
```

NLTK will handle tokenization and stopwords; spaCy will help with lemmatization and more advanced parsing.

Your First Prompt to ChatGPT

Here is a prompt that you can use exactly as it is:

Prompt to ChatGPT:

"*Generate a simple text preprocessing pipeline using* NLTK *and* spaCy *in* Python.

Include:

– *lowercasing*

– *removing punctuation*

– *removing stopwords*

– *lemmatization*

– returning a clean list of tokens.

Make the functions modular and easy to reuse.”

ChatGPT might produce something similar to what you see in the following figure:

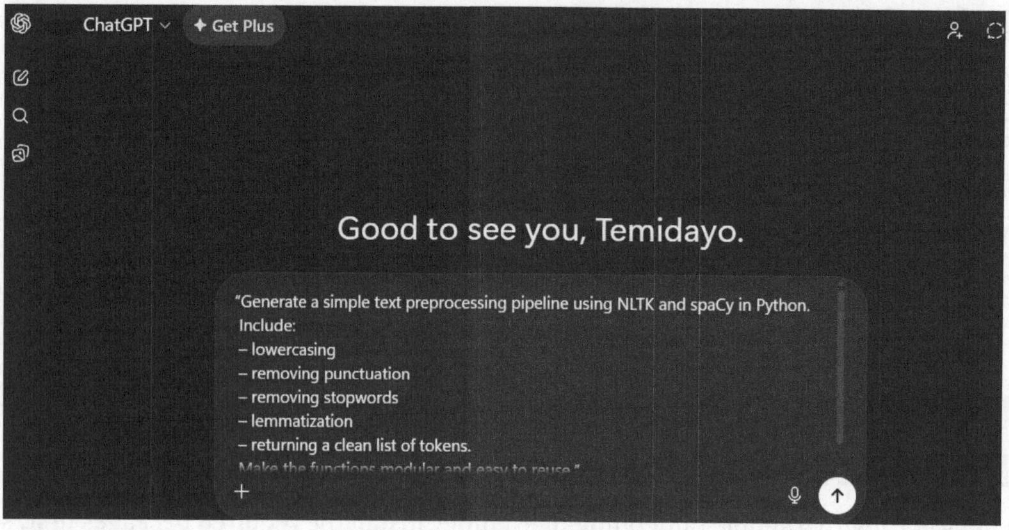

Figure 7.1: *ChatGPT Prompt*

A Clean Preprocessing Pipeline (AI-Generated)

```
import nltk
import stringimport spacy
from nltk.corpus import stopwords

# Download required NLTK data (only needed once)
nltk.download('punkt')
nltk.download('stopwords')

# Load spaCy language model
nlp = spacy.load("en_core_web_sm")

stop_words = set(stopwords.words('english'))

def preprocess_text(text):
    """
    Lowercases text, removes stop words, punctuation, and spaces,
    and returns lemmatized tokens using spaCy's native features.
    """
    doc = nlp(text.lower())

    tokens = []
```

```
    for token in doc:
        if not token.is_stop and not token.is_punct and not token.is_space:
            tokens.append(token.lemma_)

    return tokens
sample = "The Afternoon was Delightful; a rare moment of calm."
print(preprocess_text(sample))
```

When you run that code in VS Code, PyCharm, or any IDE, the output may look like:

```
['afternoon', 'delightful', 'rare', 'moment', 'calm']
```

This confirms the pipeline is working:

- punctuation removed
- stopwords removed
- words lemmatized
- casing normalized

The sentence is now represented as a clean list of core concepts.

Common Pitfalls to Avoid

Many learners trip over the same issues. So, we address them upfront:

- **Missing NLTK Downloads**

  If you see errors like:

  ```
  LookupError: Resource 'stopwords' not found.
  ```

  You simply forgot:

  ```
  nltk.download('stopwords')
  ```

- **spaCy Model Not Installed**

  If you get:

  ```
  OSError: [E050] Cannot find model 'en_core_web_sm'
  ```

  Run:

  ```
  python -m spacy download en_core_web_sm
  ```

- **Forgetting to Lowercase Text**

  Stylometric models are case-sensitive unless cleaned properly.

- **Removing Too Much**

  Over-cleaning removes style cues.

  You will learn how to balance this as we progress.

Tokenization, Stemming, and Stopword Removal with NLTK and spaCy

If you think of text preprocessing as cleaning a kitchen before cooking, then this section is about learning the **tools**, such as the knives, cutting boards, and bowls, you will reach for in every NLP project.

Tokenization, stemming, and stopword removal are the fundamentals. They help the machine understand text by breaking it down, simplifying it, and filtering out noise so that the core meaning becomes easier to analyze.

This is also where many students get stuck the first time. They try running NLP code but get errors because a library is not installed, a dataset was not downloaded, or the code behaves differently from what they expected.

So, in this section, I will guide you slowly, step by step, and show you *exactly* what you should see on your screen when you run each example.

Tokenization: Splitting Text into Words

Tokenization is the most basic building block of NLP. It is the process of breaking text into meaningful units, usually words.

You will often start by prompting ChatGPT like this:

Prompt to ChatGPT

> *"Give me Python code that tokenizes a sentence using both NLTK and spaCy. Include installation steps and show the expected output for each tokenizer."*

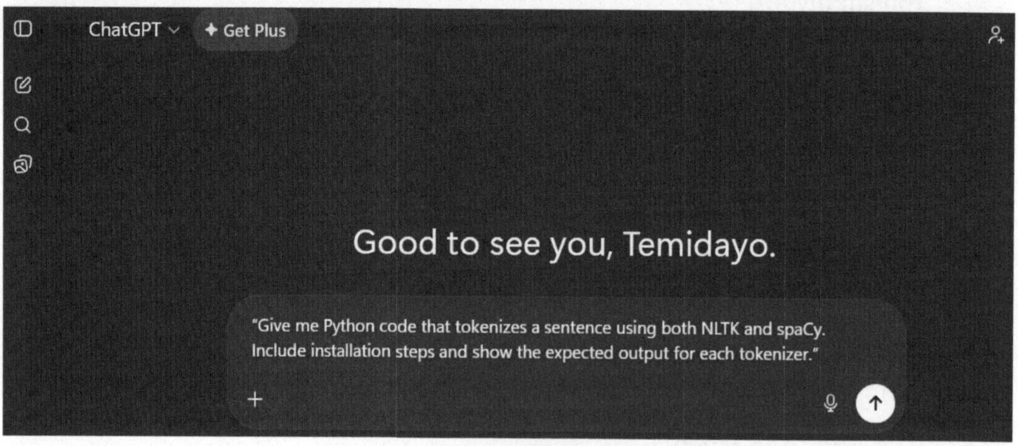

Figure 7.2: *ChatGPT Prompt*

A good response will give you something close to the following.

Tokenization with NLTK

Before running the code, install NLTK:

```
pip install nltk
```

Then run this script in your editor:

```
import nltk
nltk.download('punkt')

from nltk.tokenize import word_tokenize

text = "ChatGPT helps you write better code, faster."

tokens = word_tokenize(text)
print(tokens)
```

Expected Output

When you run this, you will likely see:

```
['ChatGPT', 'helps', 'you', 'write', 'better', 'code', ',', 'faster', '.']
```

Notice how punctuation becomes separate tokens. This is normal, and later, you will filter punctuation out.

Tokenization with spaCy

Install spaCy and its English model if you have not already:

```
pip install spacy
python -m spacy download en_core_web_sm
```

```
Then try:
import spacy

nlp = spacy.load("en_core_web_sm")
doc = nlp("ChatGPT helps you write better code, faster.")

tokens = [token.text for token in doc]
print(tokens)
```

Expected Output

```
['ChatGPT', 'helps', 'you', 'write', 'better', 'code', ',', 'faster', '.']
```

Both libraries produce similar results, but spaCy's tokenizer is more consistent and handles edge cases better (such as contractions, emojis, and hyphenated words).

Stemming: Reducing Words to Their Rough Roots

Stemming is a crude but fast way of transforming words such as:

- "running"
- "runs"
- "ran"

into a single simplified form, often "run."

It is useful when you want speed and do not need perfect grammar.

Here is the prompt:

Prompt to ChatGPT

> *"Generate a Python example using NLTK's PorterStemmer.*
>
> *Include a demonstration showing how different verb forms are stemmed."*

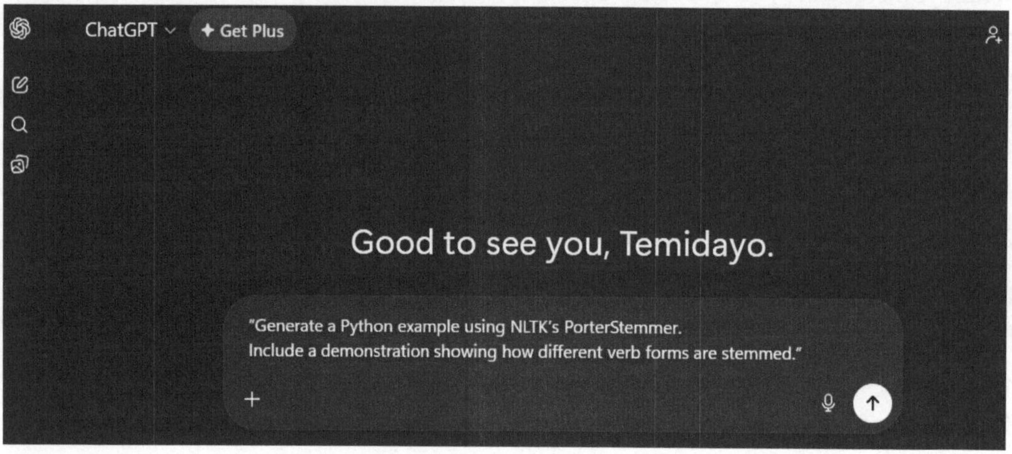

Figure 7.3: *ChatGPT Prompt*

ChatGPT should give you something similar to this.

Stemming with NLTK

```
from nltk.stem import PorterStemmer

ps = PorterStemmer()

words = ["running", "runs", "ran", "easily", "fairly"]
stems = [ps.stem(w) for w in words]

print(stems)
```

Expected Output

```
['run', 'run', 'ran', 'easili', 'fairli']
```

You will notice "easily" becomes "easili."

This is a reminder that stemming is mechanical, not linguistic.

Stopword Removal: Filtering out Noise

Stopwords are very common words such as "the," "and," "is," , and so on. They usually carry little meaning in text analysis.

Install NLTK stopwords, if needed:

```
nltk.download('stopwords')
```

```
Then:
from nltk.corpus import stopwords
from nltk.tokenize import word_tokenize

stop_words = set(stopwords.words('english'))
text = "This is a simple example to show how stopword removal works."

tokens = word_tokenize(text)
filtered = [w for w in tokens if w.lower() not in stop_words]

print(filtered)
```

Expected Output

```
['This', 'simple', 'example', 'show', 'stopword', 'removal', 'works', '.']
```

You have kept the meaning, and removed the filler.

Combining Tokenization + Stemming + Stopwords

A practical preprocessing pipeline uses several steps together.

Here is a prompt you can give to ChatGPT:

Prompt to ChatGPT

"*Write a function that takes raw text and returns a cleaned version using* NLTK:

– *lowercase everything*

– *tokenize*

– *remove stopwords*

– *apply stemming*

Show a sample output so I know what to expect.”

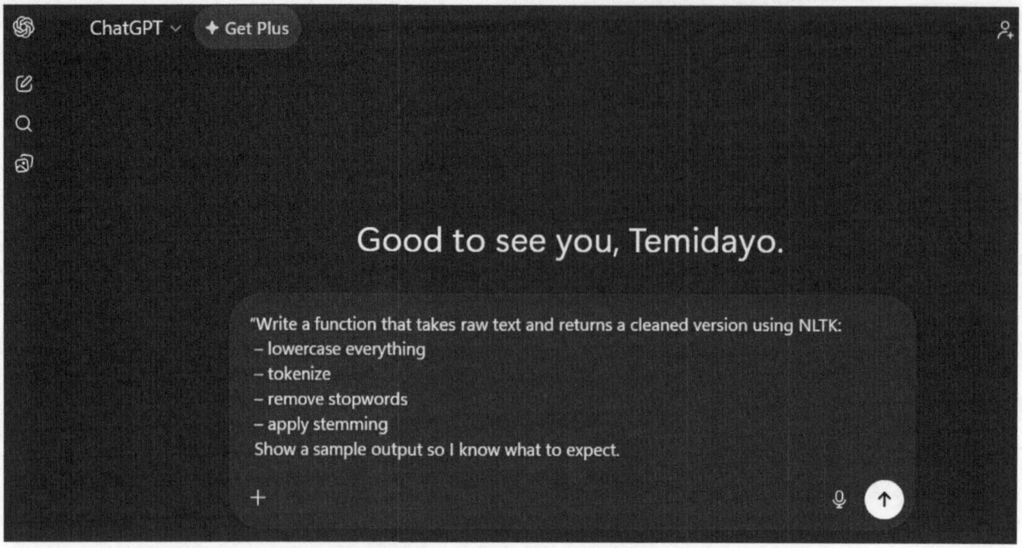

Figure 7.4: *ChatGPT Prompt*

A typical generated version will look like this:

```
import string
import nltk
from nltk.corpus import stopwords
from nltk.stem import PorterStemmer
from nltk.tokenize import word_tokenize

nltk.download(‘punkt’)
nltk.download(‘stopwords’)

stop_words = set(stopwords.words(‘english’))
ps = PorterStemmer()

def clean_text(text):
  text = text.lower()
    tokens = word_tokenize(text)

    # Remove stop words and punctuation
    tokens = [
        t for t in tokens
        if t not in stop_words and t not in string.punctuation
    ]

    stems = [ps.stem(t) for t in tokens]
    return stems
```

```
sample = "The cats were running quickly across the garden."
Print(clean_text(sample))
```

Expected Output

```
['cat', 'run', 'quickli', 'across', 'garden', '.']
```

It is rough, but clean enough for many NLP tasks.

spaCy's Alternative: Lemmatization over Stemming

spaCy does not stem, it *lemmatizes*, which gives real dictionary forms.

Add this to your understanding:

```
import spacy
nlp = spacy.load("en_core_web_sm")

doc = nlp("The cats were running quickly across the garden.")

lemmas = [token.lemma_ for token in doc if not token.is_stop and not
token.is_punct]
print(lemmas)
```

Expected Output

```
['cat', 'run', 'quickly', 'garden']
```

This is cleaner, more readable, and better suited for stylometry.

Feature Extraction: Word Frequency, N-Grams, Sentence Length

Preprocessing gives you a clean text, but clean text alone cannot tell a story.

To identify an author, a machine needs something measurable, patterns that can be compared across documents. This is where feature extraction comes in. It transforms raw text into numerical signals: frequencies, distributions, tendencies, and habits. If stylometry were detective work, features are the fingerprints left behind.

Every author tends to write sentences in a certain way. Some favor shorter phrases. Some use long and winding sentences. Some repeat specific words or patterns without realizing it.

Feature extraction captures these signatures, so that a model can learn from them.

The Foundation of Stylometry

Word frequency is one of the simplest and most powerful indicators of style. Authors have unconscious habits, such as favorite verbs, preferred transitions, and certain adjectives they reach for.

You can ask ChatGPT:

Prompt to ChatGPT

> *"Give me Python code that takes cleaned tokens and returns word frequency counts using collections.Counter. Include a sample output using a short text."*

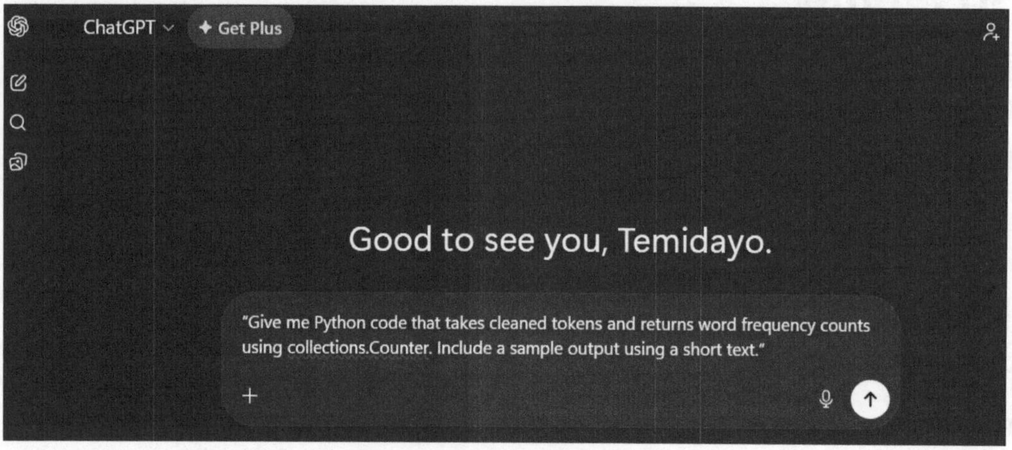

Figure 7.5: *ChatGPT Prompt*

ChatGPT will typically provide something like this.

Install nothing new—`collections are built-in.`

```
from collections import Counter
tokens = ["cat", "run", "garden", "cat", "run", "run"]
freq = Counter(tokens)
print(freq)
```

Expected Output

```
Counter({'run': 3, 'cat': 2, 'garden': 1})
```

This structure is easy to convert into features for machine learning, later.

Capturing Word Pairings and Style Patterns

Individual words tell you what an author talks about.

N-grams reveal how they string ideas together.

- **Unigrams** → `single words`
- **Bigrams** → `pairs like "in fact", "at once"`
- **Trigrams** → `triples like "as a result"`

Some authors rely heavily on certain phrases.

Ask ChatGPT:

Prompt to ChatGPT

"Generate Python code that extracts unigrams, bigrams, and trigrams from a list of tokens. Provide an example using a short sentence and show the expected output."

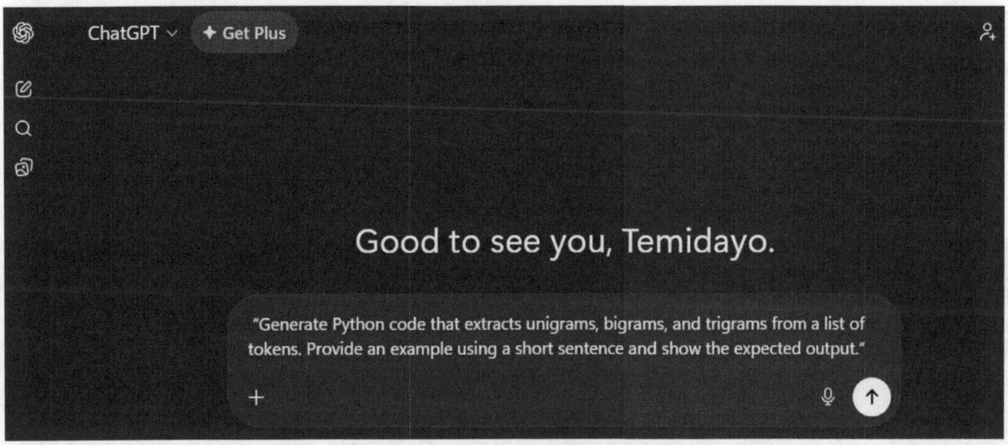

Figure 7.6: *ChatGPT Prompt*

You will often get a clean version like this:

```
from nltk.util import ngrams

tokens = ["the", "cat", "sat", "on", "the", "mat"]

unigrams = list(ngrams(tokens, 1))
bigrams = list(ngrams(tokens, 2))
trigrams = list(ngrams(tokens, 3))

print("Unigrams:", unigrams)
print("Bigrams:", bigrams)
print("Trigrams:", trigrams)
```

Expected Output

```
Unigrams: [('the',), ('cat',), ('sat',), ('on',), ('the',), ('mat',)]
Bigrams: [('the', 'cat'), ('cat', 'sat'), ('sat', 'on'), ('on', 'the'),
('the', 'mat')]
```

```
Trigrams: [('the', 'cat', 'sat'), ('cat', 'sat', 'on'), ('sat', 'on',
'the'), ('on', 'the', 'mat')]
```

These patterns often make excellent features for authorship identification, especially when comparing two or more writers.

Measuring Rhythm and Flow

Sentence length, both in words and characters, is another strong stylistic marker. Some authors write short and clipped sentences. Others write dense ones with long and layered structures.

Before extracting sentence lengths, split the text into sentences.

Ask ChatGPT:

Prompt to ChatGPT

> *"Provide Python code that splits text into sentences using NLTK's `sent_tokenize`, then computes sentence lengths. Show the expected output."*

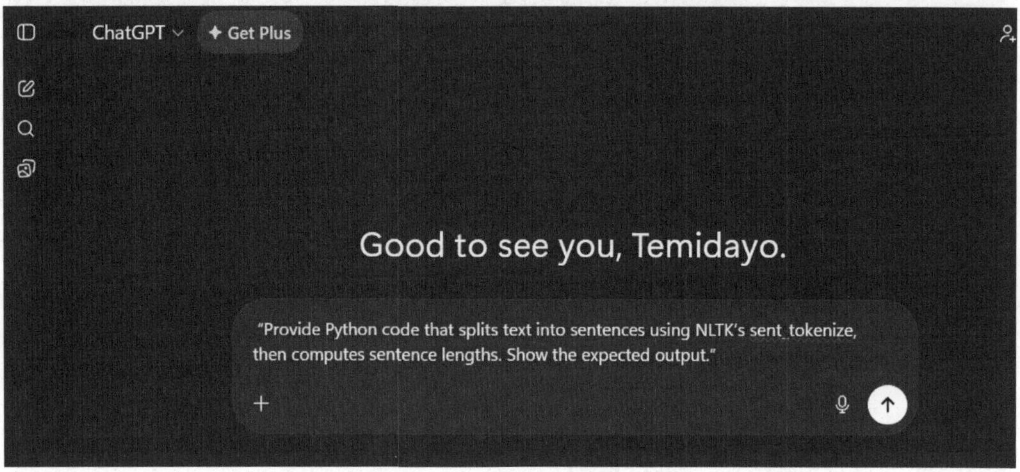

***Figure** 7.7: ChatGPT Prompt*

Sentence Length Extraction

```
Install if needed:
pip install nltk
```

Download the Sentence Tokenizer:

```
import nltk
nltk.download('punkt')
```

Then:

```
from nltk.tokenize import sent_tokenize, word_tokenize
text = "This is the first sentence. Here is another one, slightly longer.
And a third."
Sentences = sent_tokenize(text)

lengths = [len(word_tokenize(s)) for s in sentences]

print("Sentences:", sentences)
print("Lengths:", lengths)
```

Expected Output

```
Sentences: ['This is the first sentence.', 'Here is another one, slightly
longer.', 'And a third.']
Lengths: [6, 7, 3]
```

These values will later feed directly into your model as numerical features.

Combining All Extracted Features into a Single Pipeline

At this stage, your program will start to resemble real-world NLP pipelines.

Here is a prompt you can use:

Prompt to ChatGPT

"Write a `extract_features(text)` function that:

- tokenizes

- removes stopwords

- lemmatizes (spaCy)

- extracts word frequencies

- extracts bigrams

- calculates sentence lengths

Return all features in a dictionary.

Show example output."

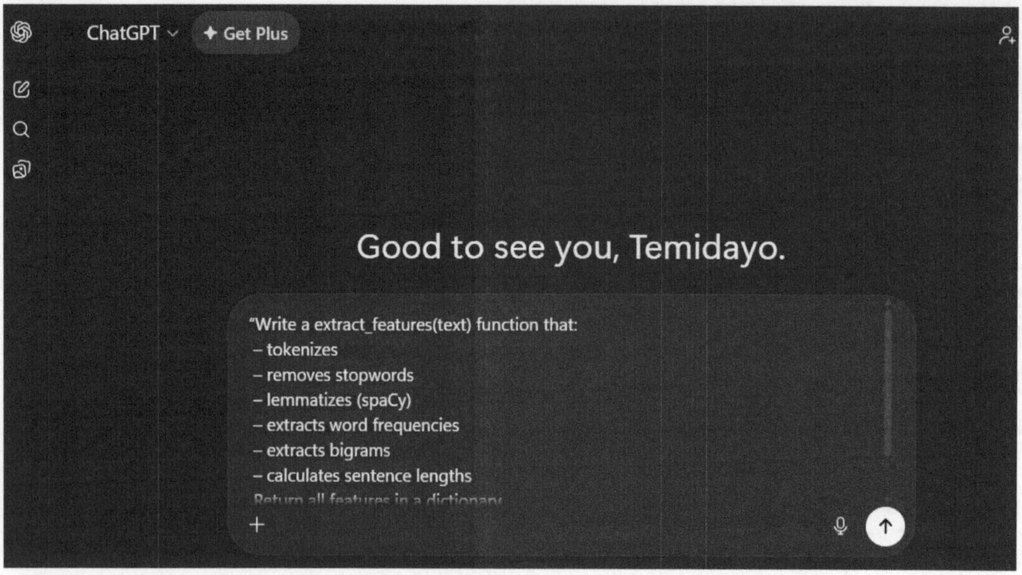

Figure 7.8: *ChatGPT Prompt*

Expect Something Like This:

```
import spacy
from collections import Counter

nlp = spacy.load("en_core_web_sm")

def extract_features(text):
    # Run the spaCy pipeline once
    doc = nlp(text)

    # Token-level features
    tokens = [
        token.lemma_.lower()
        for token in doc
        if not token.is_stop and not token.is_punct
    ]

    freq = Counter(tokens)

    # Bigrams
    bigrams = list(zip(tokens, tokens[1:]))

    # Sentence lengths (reuse spaCy's sentence segmentation)
    lengths = [len(sent) for sent in doc.sents]

    return {
```

```
        "frequencies": freq,
        "bigrams": bigrams,
        "sentence_lengths": lengths,    }

sample = "The cat sat on the mat. The cat looked outside."
print(extract_features(sample))
```

Expected Output (Structure Varies)

```
{
 'frequencies': Counter({'cat': 2, 'sit': 1, 'mat': 1, 'look': 1,
'outside': 1}),
 'bigrams': [('cat', 'sit'), ('sit', 'mat'), ('cat', 'look'), ('look',
'outside')],
 'sentence_lengths': [6, 5]
}
```

Training a Simple Classifier for Authorship Detection (scikit-learn)

Feature extraction gives you the raw ingredients; now it is time to teach a machine to notice the differences between writers. This is where a classifier steps in. Your job is to convert stylometric patterns, such as frequencies, n-grams, and sentence lengths, into numerical vectors that a model can understand, then train it to recognize which author each pattern belongs to.

Preparing Data for Training

Before training a model, you need examples of writing from each author. For practice, you can start with small text samples, two or three authors with a handful of paragraphs each.

A simple dataset structure might look like this:

```
data/
 ├── austen_1.txt
 ├── austen_2.txt
 ├── twain_1.txt
 ├── twain_2.txt
 └── poe_1.txt
```

Each file contains a short excerpt.

If you want ChatGPT to scaffold your dataset loader, you can use this prompt:

Prompt to ChatGPT

> *"Create Python code that loads all .txt files in a folder, assigns author labels based on filename prefixes (e.g., `austen_*.txt`), and stores them in a DataFrame with text and author columns."*

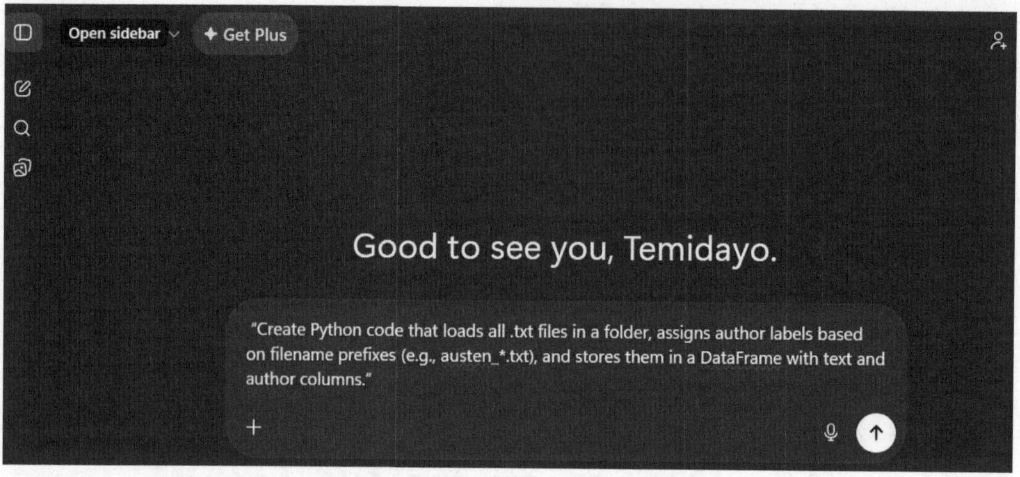

Figure 7.9: *ChatGPT Prompt*

Here is the kind of response you should expect.

Loading Text Samples into a DataFrame

```
Install pandas if needed:
pip install pandas

import os
import pandas as pd

def load_dataset(folder):
    records = []

    for fname in os.listdir(folder):
        if fname.endswith(".txt"):
            author = fname.split("_")[0]   # austen_1.txt → "austen"
            with open(os.path.join(folder, fname), "r",
encoding="utf-8") as f:
                text = f.read()
            records.append({"author": author, "text": text})

    return pd.DataFrame(records)

df = load_dataset("data")
print(df.head())
```

Expected Output

```
  author          text
0  austen  It is a truth universally acknowledged...
1  austen  Elizabeth's spirits soon rising to playfulness...
2  twain   Persons attempting to find a motive in this...
3  twain   The secret of getting ahead is getting started...
4  poe     Once upon a midnight dreary, while I pondered...
```

This structure is all you need to start training!

Converting Features into Numerical Vectors

Machine Learning (ML) models in scikit-learn expect numerical vectors. Fortunately, scikit-learn already provides tools to extract text-based features from raw text, such as:

- **`CountVectorizer`**: word counts,
- **`TfidfVectorizer`**: weighted word importance, and
- **N-gram Extraction.**

For authorship tasks, TF-IDF usually works well. Pair it with your custom features, later.

Ask ChatGPT:

Prompt to ChatGPT

> *"Write code that uses TfidfVectorizer to turn the text column into feature vectors. Use unigrams and bigrams. Show the resulting shape of the vectorized dataset."*

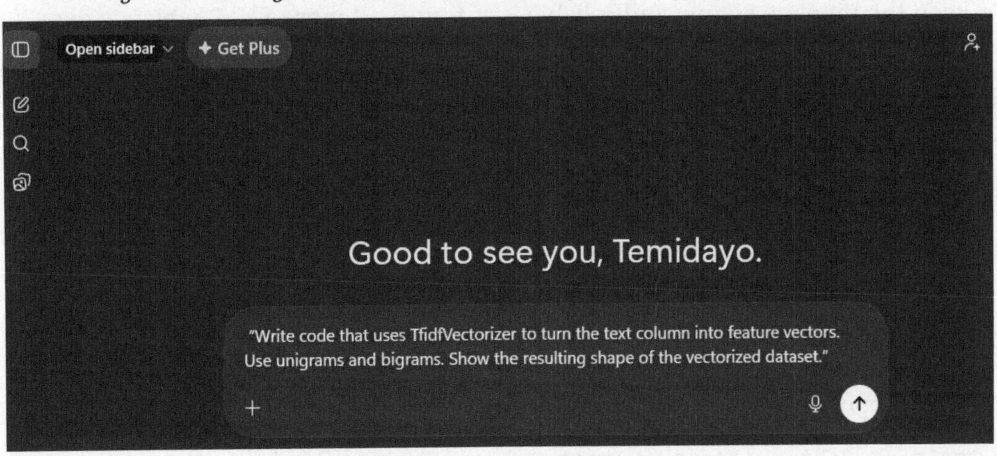

Figure 7.10: ChatGPT Prompt

Example Output:

Vectorizing Text with TF-IDF

```
Install scikit-learn if needed:
pip install scikit-learn

from sklearn.feature_extraction.text import TfidfVectorizer

vectorizer = TfidfVectorizer(ngram_range=(1, 2), min_df=2)
X = vectorizer.fit_transform(df["text"])
y = df["author"]

print("Feature matrix shape:", X.shape)
```

Expected Output

```
Feature matrix shape: (12, 1950)
```

- **12 documents and**
- **1,950 features** extracted from their wording patterns.

The model now has something numerical to learn from.

Training a Classifier

For authorship identification, many algorithms work well:

- Logistic Regression,
- Linear SVM, and
- Multinomial Naive Bayes.

To keep the pipeline simple and reliable, start with a **Linear SVM**, which is excellent for text tasks.

Here is a prompt you can use:

Prompt to ChatGPT

> *"Generate Python code that trains a LinearSVC classifier on TF-IDF vectors and prints accuracy using train-test split."*

You will receive something like:

```
from sklearn.model_selection import train_test_split
from sklearn.svm import LinearSVC
from sklearn.metrics import accuracy_score

X_train, X_test, y_train, y_test = train_test_split(
    X, y, test_size=0.25, random_state=42
)
```

```
model = LinearSVC()
model.fit(X_train, y_train)

preds = model.predict(X_test)

print("Accuracy:", accuracy_score(y_test, preds))
```

Expected Output

```
Accuracy: 0.75
```

Your accuracy will vary depending on how distinct your authors are, and how much text you provide.

The important part is that you now have a trainable and testable classification pipeline.

Predicting the Author of a New Text

Once trained, the model can classify a new writing.

Ask ChatGPT:

Prompt to ChatGPT

> *"Write a function predict_author(text) that applies the same* TF-IDF *vectorizer to new text and uses the trained classifier to return the predicted author."*

Prediction Function

```
def predict_author(text):
    vec = vectorizer.transform([text])
    return model.predict(vec)[0]

sample = "It was a dreary night when I first beheld the accomplishment of
my toils."
print("Predicted author:", predict_author(sample))
```

Expected Output

```
Predicted author: poe
```

Conclusion

In this chapter, you built a simple but powerful authorship identification program using Natural Language Processing (NLP).

You learned how to extract writing-style features, convert text into numerical form, train a machine learning model, and test whether it can correctly predict the author of a given text.

In the next chapter, you will learn how to automatically generate data summaries, charts, and simple reports using Python and ChatGPT. This is especially useful for analysts, business users, and anyone handling spreadsheets.

Points to Remember

- Authorship identification uses writing patterns to guess who wrote a text.
- NLP transforms messy text into structured data that the model can learn from.
- You can extract features like word count, vocabulary richness, punctuation use, and sentence length.
- Clean and preprocessed text improves model performance dramatically.
- Real-world NLP needs more data, but your small project still simulates a real industry workflow.

Key Terms

- **NLP (Natural Language Processing):** Techniques that help computers understand human language.
- **Vectorization:** Turning text into numbers that the machine can learn from.
- **Feature Extraction:** Pulling important characteristics from text (for example, word frequency).
- **Training Set:** Data the model learns from.
- **Classifier:** A model that predicts categories (such as an author's name).
- **Accuracy Score:** A measure of how well your model performs.

Task to Complete

Create your own small authorship dataset with at least two authors (you can write the samples yourself). Then, build a simple NLP classifier that tries to predict the author of a new text.

Your task must include the following:

- Writing or collecting at least 6 text samples per author
- Splitting into training/testing data
- Vectorizing the text
- Training a classifier
- Testing accuracy
- Printing the prediction for at least two new text samples

CHAPTER 8
Automating Data Reports

Introduction

Reports are the lifeblood of decision-making. Whether it is tracking sales, analyzing website traffic, or reviewing project performance, stakeholders rely on clear, accurate, and timely reports to make informed choices. Yet, if you have ever created a weekly report from scratch, you know how much time is wasted on repetitive tasks. Hours can slip away before the first meaningful insight is even written.

Throughout this chapter, you will see how AI can accelerate your workflow and help you think about the best way to structure your pipeline, suggest efficient libraries, and even propose narrative summaries for your data findings. The end goal is not to replace your analytical judgment but to free you from tedious work, so that you can focus on insights.

Structure

In this chapter, we will cover the following topics:

- Using AI to Generate Scripts for Data Ingestion and Cleaning
- Summarizing Data with Pandas and NumPy
- Data Visualization with Matplotlib and Seaborn
- Exporting Reports as PDF/Excel with ReportLab and openpyxl
- Hands-on Project: Build an Automated Weekly Sales or Performance Report Pipeline

Using AI to Generate Scripts for Data Ingestion and Cleaning

Before we can analyze data or create visualizations, the raw information must first be ingested and cleaned. In real-world scenarios, datasets are rarely perfect. Missing values, inconsistent formats, duplicate rows, and extraneous columns are all part of the challenge. Doing this manually, especially on large datasets, can be tedious and error-prone.

With Python and ChatGPT, you can streamline these tasks into reusable scripts.

Data Ingestion

Python provides multiple ways to ingest data. Depending on your source, you may use:

- `pandas.read_csv()` for CSV files
- `pandas.read_excel()` for Excel sheets
- `requests or urllib` for fetching data from APIs or web endpoints
- `sqlite3` or `SQLAlchemy` for database connections

Example Prompt for ChatGPT:

"*Generate a Python script that reads a CSV file called* `sales_data.csv`*, ensures that the date column is parsed as a* `datetime object`*, and prints the first 10 rows.*"

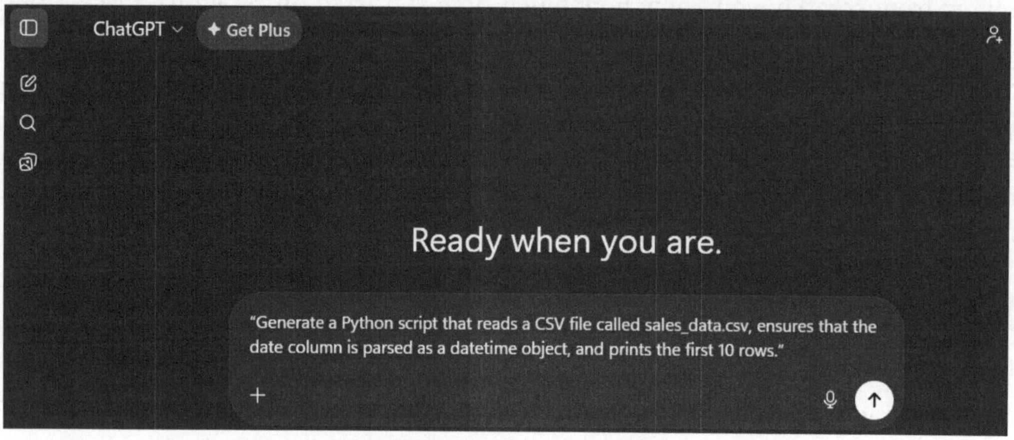

Figure 8.1: *ChatGPT Prompt*

Sample Output from ChatGPT:

```
import pandas as pd

# Read CSV and parse dates
df = pd.read_csv('sales_data.csv', parse_dates=['date'])

# Preview the first 10 rows
print(df.head(10))
```

This snippet is ready to run in VS Code, once you install the pandas:

```
pip install pandas
```

Notice how the prompt specifies the dataset, column types, and preview step. This clarity ensures that the generated code matches your intent.

Cleaning the Data

After ingestion, the next step is **cleaning**. Typical operations include:

- Handling missing values (`NaN`)
- Dropping duplicates
- Renaming columns for consistency
- Correcting data types

Example Prompt for ChatGPT:

> *"Clean `sales_data.csv` by removing duplicates, filling missing values in the `revenue` column with 0, and standardizing column names to lowercase with underscores."*

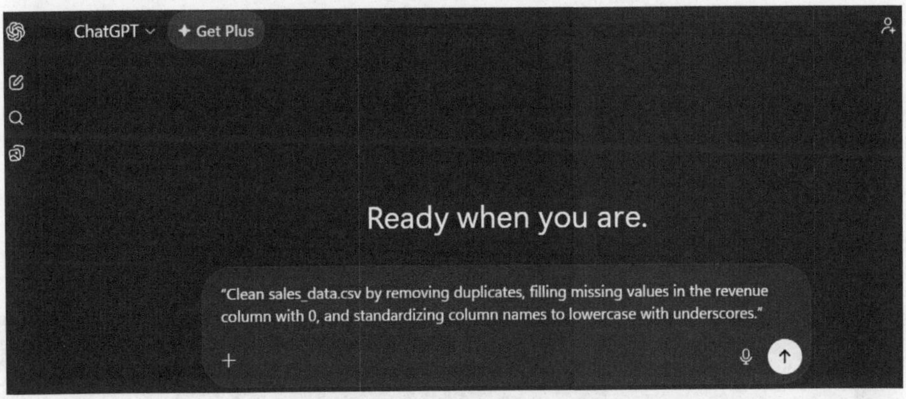

Figure 8.2: *ChatGPT Prompt*

Sample Output from ChatGPT:

```
# Drop duplicates
df = df.drop_duplicates()

# Fill missing revenue values
df['revenue'] = df['revenue'].fillna(0)

# Standardize column names
df.columns = [col.strip().lower().replace(' ', '_') for col in
df.columns]

print(df.info())
```

This example demonstrates how ChatGPT can turn plain-language instructions into executable Python code, eliminating repetitive tasks while maintaining your control over the process.

Validating the Data

Even after AI generates code, it is essential to validate the results. Some questions to ask yourself:

- Are all necessary columns present?
- Are data types correct?
- Did the cleaning step inadvertently remove important rows?

You can include simple checks in your script:

```
# Check for missing values
print(df.isnull().sum())

# Confirm data types
print(df.dtypes)
```

Creating Reusable Functions

A powerful pattern is to wrap ingestion and cleaning steps into functions. ChatGPT can assist in generating these:

Prompt Example:

> "*Create a Python function* `load_and_clean_csv(file_path)` *that reads a CSV, fills missing* `revenue` *with 0, removes duplicates, and standardizes column names.*"

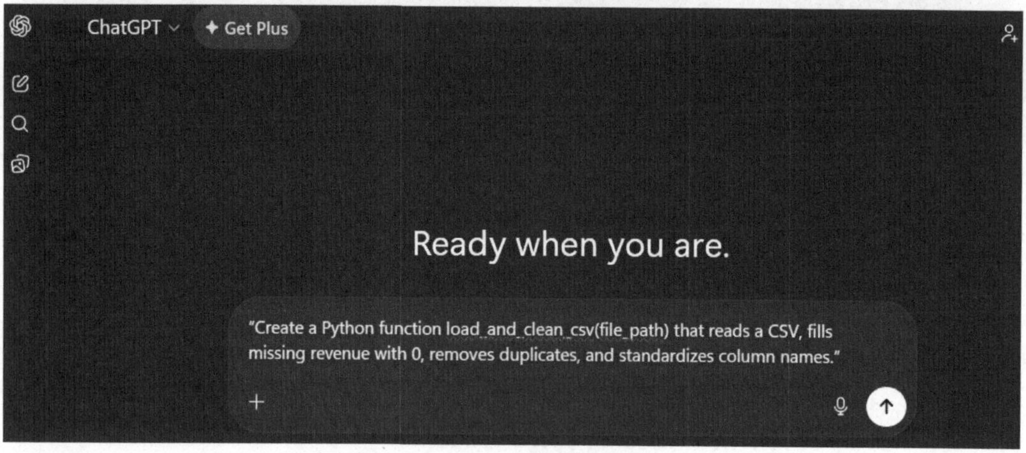

Figure 8.3: *ChatGPT Prompt*

Sample Output:

```
import pandas as pd

def load_and_clean_csv(file_path):
```

```
    df = pd.read_csv(file_path, parse_dates=['date'])
    df = df.drop_duplicates()
    df['revenue'] = df['revenue'].fillna(0)
    df.columns = [col.strip().lower().replace(' ', '_') for col in
df.columns]
    return df

# Usage
df = load_and_clean_csv('sales_data.csv')
print(df.head())
```

This function can now be reused for multiple datasets without rewriting the code.

Hands-on Tips while Following the Rules

- Always inspect the first few rows of your dataset (**`df.head()`**) after ingestion.
- Keep a copy of the raw data untouched, so that you can restart, if cleaning goes wrong.
- Encourage ChatGPT to **explain each step**, if you are unsure why it is doing something. For example:

"*Explain why we are using `fillna(0)`, and when this might not be appropriate.*"

This builds understanding, not just automation.

Summarizing Data with Pandas and NumPy

Once your data is ingested and cleaned, the next step is summarization. In real-world projects, raw data rarely tells the story at first glance. You need to compute aggregates, detect trends, and extract key insights before presenting findings or creating reports. Python's **`pandas`** and **`NumPy`** libraries are perfect for this.

Using ChatGPT, you can quickly generate scripts that provide these summaries, while learning why each step matters. The focus here is on interpretation and reusability, rather than just copying the codes.

Using Pandas for Quick Summaries

Pandas makes it simple to explore the data. Some core operations include:

- `df.describe() - summary statistics for numeric columns`
- `df['column'].value_counts() - counts of unique values`
- `df.groupby('column').agg() - aggregation by category][][`

Prompt Example for ChatGPT:

"Generate a Python script using pandas that summarizes `sales_data.csv`*, showing total revenue per region, average revenue per product category, and counts of transactions per month."*

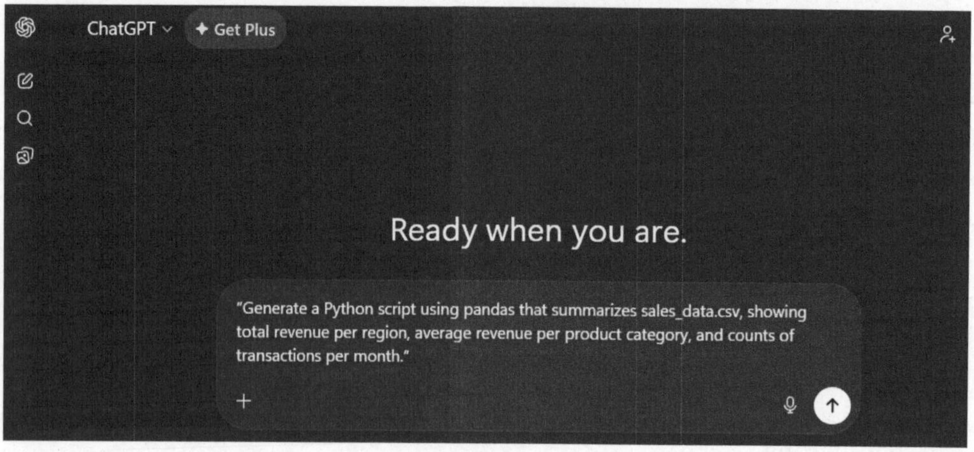

Figure 8.4: *ChatGPT Prompt*

Sample Output from ChatGPT:

```
import pandas as pd

# Load cleaned data
df = pd.read_csv('sales_data_cleaned.csv', parse_dates=['date'])

# Total revenue per region
total_revenue = df.groupby('region')['revenue'].sum()
print("Total Revenue per Region:\n", total_revenue)

# Average revenue per product category
avg_revenue = df.groupby('product_category')['revenue'].mean()
print("\nAverage Revenue per Product Category:\n", avg_revenue)

# Transactions per month (DatetimeIndex-friendly)
df['month'] = df['date'].dt.to_period('M').dt.to_timestamp()
transactions_per_month = df.groupby('month').size()
print("\nTransactions per Month:\n", transactions_per_month)
```

Key Points:

- ChatGPT can suggest aggregations based on **column types and business context**.
- Using `groupby + agg` allows flexibility in summarizing multiple metrics.
- Always inspect results with `print()` or `head()` for sanity checks.

Incorporating NumPy for Numerical Insights

NumPy can complement pandas when you need mathematical or statistical operations such as sums, means, medians, standard deviations, or complex computations.

Prompt Example for ChatGPT:

> *"Write Python code using NumPy to compute the mean, median, and standard deviation of the revenue column in `sales_data_cleaned.csv`."*

Sample Output:

```
import numpy as np

# Convert revenue column to NumPy array
revenue = df['revenue'].to_numpy()

mean_revenue = np.mean(revenue)
median_revenue = np.median(revenue)
std_revenue = np.std(revenue)

print(f"Mean Revenue: {mean_revenue}")
print(f"Median Revenue: {median_revenue}")
print(f"Revenue Std Dev: {std_revenue}")
```

Hands-on Tips:

- Compare pandas and NumPy outputs; both are valid, but pandas integrate better with labeled data.
- ChatGPT can guide you on **vectorized operations**, which are faster than loops for large datasets.
- Always validate calculations for accuracy, especially after cleaning steps.

Creating a Summarized Table for Reporting

After computing metrics, you might want to create a single summarized table combining multiple insights:

Prompt Example:

> *"Generate a summary table for `sales_data_cleaned.csv` that includes total revenue, average revenue, and number of transactions per region."*

Sample Output:

```
summary = df.groupby('region').agg(
    total_revenue=pd.NamedAgg(column='revenue', aggfunc='sum'),
    avg_revenue=pd.NamedAgg(column='revenue', aggfunc='mean'),
```

```
    transaction_count=pd.NamedAgg(column='revenue', aggfunc='count')
)

print(summary)
```

This table is now ready to feed into a report generator such as Excel, PDF, or a visualization.

Prompting Best Practices

When asking ChatGPT to summarize data:

- **Be specific**: mention the dataset, columns, and desired metrics.
- **Include business context**: for example, "per region", "per month", or "per product category."
- **Ask ChatGPT to explain each line of the code**: this reinforces learning, instead of just copying snippets.

Example Prompt for Explanation:

> "*Explain each line of this Python code for summarizing* `sales_data.csv`, *and why each aggregation is used.*"

Data Visualization with Matplotlib and Seaborn

Numbers rarely convince on their own. They need shape, contrast, and context. A table of averages can inform, but a chart can persuade. In automated reporting, visualization is the bridge between analysis and understanding. This section focuses on building that bridge carefully using Python, guided by well-structured prompts to ChatGPT.

Why Visualization Comes after Summarization

At this point in the chapter, you already have:

- Cleaned data
- Aggregated metrics
- Summary tables

Visualization is not exploratory guessing anymore. It is intentional communication.

Before writing any code, ask yourself:

- What question should this chart answer?

- Who is the report for?
- What decision might follow from this image?

This thinking shapes how you prompt ChatGPT.

Installing Required Libraries

Before continuing, ensure that these libraries are installed in your environment:

```
pip install matplotlib seaborn pandas numpy
```

If you have already installed `pandas` and `numpy`, this command will only add what is missing.

The Foundation

Matplotlib is the base plotting library in Python. It gives you full control but expects you to be explicit.

Let us start with a simple use case: monthly revenue trends.

Prompting ChatGPT Effectively

Instead of asking:

> *"Plot revenue data"*

Ask:

> *"Generate a Python script using matplotlib that plots the total monthly revenue as a line chart from `sales_data_cleaned.csv`. The x-axis should be months, the y-axis total revenue, and the chart should be labeled clearly for reporting."*

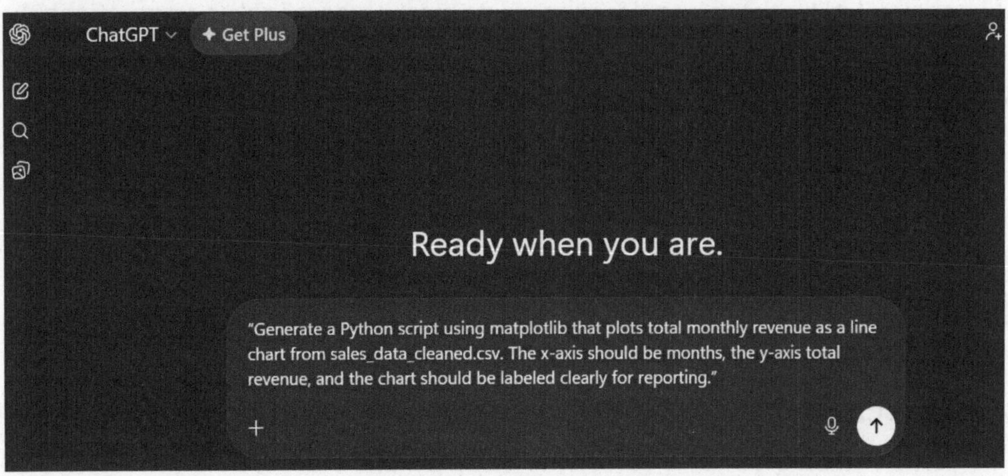

Figure 8.5: *ChatGPT Prompt*

Sample Code ChatGPT May Generate:

```
import pandas as pd
import matplotlib.pyplot as plt
df = pd.read_csv('sales_data_cleaned.csv', parse_dates=['date'])
df['month'] = df['date'].dt.to_period('M')
monthly_revenue = df.groupby('month')['revenue'].sum()
plt.figure()
monthly_revenue.plot(kind='line')
plt.xlabel('Month')
plt.ylabel('Total Revenue')
plt.title('Monthly Revenue Trend')
plt.tight_layout()
plt.show()
```

Sample Output (IDE)

- A clean line chart showing revenue rising or falling over time.
- X-axis labeled by month.
- Y-axis showing revenue values.

This chart answers one question clearly:

How is revenue changing over time?

Clarity and Defaults

Seaborn sits on top of matplotlib. It reduces boilerplate, and produces cleaner visuals by default.

Where matplotlib asks you to describe everything, seaborn makes assumptions that usually work well for reports.

When to Prefer Seaborn:

- Comparing categories
- Showing distributions
- Visualizing grouped summaries

Bar Charts for Categorical Comparisons

Suppose, you want to show the total revenue per region.

Prompt to ChatGPT

> *"Write Python code using seaborn to visualize the total revenue per region from `sales_data_cleaned.csv` as a bar chart suitable for a business report."*

Sample Code Output

```
import seaborn as sns
import matplotlib.pyplot as plt

# df is assumed to be already loaded and cleaned in a previous step
# Uncomment the line below only if running this code independently
# df = pd.read_csv('sales_data_cleaned.csv')

region_summary = df.groupby('region', as_index=False)['revenue'].sum()

plt.figure()
sns.barplot(data=region_summary, x='region', y='revenue')
plt.xlabel('Region')
plt.ylabel('Total Revenue')
plt.title('Total Revenue by Region')
plt.tight_layout()
plt.show()
```

What You Should Notice

- No loops.
- No manual bar calculations.
- Seaborn handles alignment and spacing.
- The visualization reads naturally left to right.

This is exactly what automated reporting needs: predictable and readable output.

Visualizing Distributions

Aggregates can hide important patterns. Sometimes, you need to see how values spread.

Example: Revenue per transaction.

Prompt

> *"Generate a seaborn histogram showing the distribution of revenue per transaction in `sales_data_cleaned.csv`. Include appropriate labels."*

Sample Code

```
plt.figure()
sns.histplot(df['revenue'], bins=30)
plt.xlabel('Revenue per Transaction')
plt.ylabel('Frequency')
plt.title('Distribution of Revenue per Transaction')
```

```
plt.tight_layout()
plt.show()
```

This chart helps to answer the following questions:

- Are most transactions small or large?
- Are there outliers that affect averages?

Combining Summaries with Visuals

One of the strongest workflows in automated reporting is:

1. Summarize data with pandas
2. Visualize the summary
3. Export the result

You can ask ChatGPT to connect these steps deliberately.

Example Prompt

> *"Create a Python script that summarizes average monthly revenue and visualizes it using seaborn in a line chart. Explain each step."*

This reinforces learning, and avoids blind copying.

Exporting Reports as PDF and Excel with ReportLab and openpyxl

At some point, charts on your screen stop being useful. Stakeholders do not open VS Code. They open email attachments. They expect files they can archive, forward, and review without explanation. This is where automation becomes real, when your script produces a finished report without manual formatting or copy-pasting.

Installing the Required Libraries

Before writing any export logic, install the necessary packages:

```
pip install openpyxl reportlab
```

If you plan to embed charts as images later, you will also need:

```
pip install pillow
```

Do not skip this step. Missing libraries are the most common reason, report scripts fail.

Choosing the Right Output Format

Different formats serve different purposes:

- **Excel (`.xlsx`)**

  Best for:

  - Interactive review
  - Further filtering
  - Finance and operations teams

- **PDF (`.pdf`)**

  Best for:

  - Executive summaries
  - Fixed layouts
  - Official reporting

Your automation pipeline can generate both from the same dataset.

Exporting Data to Excel with openpyxl

Let us start with Excel, since it fits naturally with pandas.

Prompting ChatGPT Properly

Instead of:

> "*Save dataframe to Excel.*"

Ask:

> "*Generate a Python script that exports summary statistics and charts to an Excel file using openpyxl. The file should include a summary sheet and a data sheet.*"

This tells ChatGPT that you are thinking beyond raw data.

Writing Structured Excel Reports

Example: Exporting Summary and Raw Data

```
import pandas as pd

df = pd.read_csv('sales_data_cleaned.csv')
summary = df.groupby('region')['revenue'].sum().reset_index()

with pd.ExcelWriter('weekly_sales_report.xlsx', engine='openpyxl') as
writer:
```

```
    df.to_excel(writer, sheet_name='Raw Data', index=False)
    summary.to_excel(writer, sheet_name='Revenue by Region', index=False)
```

In the project folder:

- `weekly_sales_report.xlsx`
- Two sheets:
    - **Raw Data**
    - **Revenue by Region**

This is already usable. But we can improve it.

Formatting Excel Reports with openpyxl

Pandas writes data. openpyxl styles it.

Prompt to ChatGPT

> *"Extend the Excel export script to format headers in bold and auto-adjust column widths using openpyxl."*

Sample Code Extension

```
from openpyxl import load_workbook
from openpyxl.styles import Font

wb = load_workbook('weekly_sales_report.xlsx')
ws = wb['Revenue by Region']

for cell in ws[1]:
    cell.font = Font(bold=True)

for column in ws.columns:
    max_length = max(len(str(cell.value)) for cell in column)
    ws.column_dimensions[column[0].column_letter].width = max_length + 2

wb.save('weekly_sales_report.xlsx')
```

Now, your report looks intentional rather than machine-generated.

Exporting Reports to PDF with ReportLab

PDF reports require more structure. You are no longer dumping data; you are composing a document.

ReportLab builds PDFs using:

- Paragraphs
- Tables

- Flowable Elements

It rewards planning.

Prompting ChatGPT for PDF Generation

A weak prompt:

> *"Create a PDF report."*

A useful prompt:

> *"Write a Python script using ReportLab that generates a PDF sales report with a title, summary paragraph, and a table showing revenue by region."*

Creating a Basic PDF Report

```
from reportlab.platypus import SimpleDocTemplate, Paragraph, Table
from reportlab.lib.styles import getSampleStyleSheet
import pandas as pd

summary = pd.read_csv('sales_data_cleaned.csv') \
          .groupby('region')['revenue'] \
          .sum() \
          .reset_index()

doc = SimpleDocTemplate("weekly_sales_report.pdf")
styles = getSampleStyleSheet()
elements = []

elements.append(Paragraph("Weekly Sales Report", styles['Title']))
elements.append(Paragraph(
    "This report summarizes revenue performance by region for the current 
week.",
    styles['Normal']
))

table_data = [summary.columns.tolist()] + summary.values.tolist()
elements.append(Table(table_data))

doc.build(elements)
```

Output You Will See:

- A PDF file named **`weekly_sales_report.pdf`**
- Title at the top
- Short explanation
- Clean the table of the summarized data

Adding Charts to PDFs

Charts created with matplotlib or seaborn can be saved and embedded.

Save the Chart

```
plt.savefig("revenue_by_region.png")
```

Embed into PDF

```
from reportlab.platypus import Image

elements.append(Image("revenue_by_region.png", width=400, height=300))
```

Thus, ChatGPT can help you tune layout dimensions, but always run and inspect the output.

Building an Automated Weekly Sales (or Performance) Report Pipeline

This is where everything you have learned in this chapter finally comes together.

Up to now, we have worked in pieces: loading data, cleaning it, summarizing it, visualizing it, and exporting reports. In real work, these steps are not separate files or experiments. They live inside one dependable pipeline that runs every week without drama.

In this section, you will build that pipeline end-to-end.

What We are Building

By the end of this project, you will have a Python script that:

1. Loads weekly sales or performance data
2. Cleans and validates the data
3. Generates summary metrics
4. Creates visual charts
5. Exports:
    - An Excel report
    - A PDF report
6. Is structured, so that it can be scheduled to run weekly.

You can reuse this pipeline for:

- Sales reports
- Website analytics
- Employee performance summaries
- Operational metrics

Only the data source changes.

Project Setup

Folder Structure

Create a project folder like this:

```
weekly_report/
│
├── data/
│   └── sales_data.csv
│
├── output/
│   ├── reports/
│   └── charts/
│
├── report_pipeline.py
└── requirements.txt
```

This structure matters. It keeps automation predictable.

Required Libraries

Install everything before writing the code:

```
pip install pandas numpy matplotlib seaborn openpyxl reportlab
```

If anything fails, fix it now. Automation fails early or fails later; please choose early.

Step 1: Define the Problem Clearly (Before Coding)

Before touching the code, pause and write this sentence for yourself:

> *"Each week, I want a script that takes raw sales data, and produces a finished report without manual steps."*

This sentence will guide your prompts.

Step 2: Load and Inspect the Data

Assume **`sales_data.csv`** contains:

```
date,region,product,revenue
2025-01-01,West,Product A,1200
2025-01-02,East,Product B,950
```

Prompt to ChatGPT

> *"Write Python code that loads a CSV sales dataset, parses dates correctly, and displays basic info to verify data integrity."*

Code

```
import pandas as pd

df = pd.read_csv("data/sales_data.csv", parse_dates=["date"])

print(df.head())
print(df.info())
```

What You Should See

- A preview of the data.
- Confirmation that dates are parsed correctly.
- No missing columns.

If something looks wrong here, the report is already broken.

Step 3: Clean and Validate the Data

Real data is messy. Automation assumes that mess exists.

Prompt to ChatGPT

> *"Extend the script to clean sales data by removing missing revenue values, and ensuring revenue is numeric."*

Code

```
df["revenue"] = pd.to_numeric(df["revenue"], errors="coerce")
df = df.dropna(subset=["revenue"])
```

You are not fixing data for perfection. You are fixing it for consistency.

Step 4: Generate Weekly Summary Metrics

Now, we summarize what matters.

Prompt to ChatGPT

> *"Generate Python code that summarizes the total weekly revenue by region."*

Code

```
weekly_summary = (
    df.groupby("region")["revenue"]
    .sum()
    .reset_index()
)
```

This single table is the backbone of the report.

Step 5: Create Visualizations

Charts turn numbers into decisions.

Prompt to ChatGPT

> *"Create a bar chart showing the total revenue by region using matplotlib or seaborn, and save it as an image."*

Code

```
import matplotlib.pyplot as plt
import seaborn as sns

plt.figure(figsize=(8, 5))
sns.barplot(data=weekly_summary, x="region", y="revenue")
plt.title("Weekly Revenue by Region")
plt.tight_layout()
plt.savefig("output/charts/revenue_by_region.png")
plt.close()
```

What You Should See

- A PNG chart saved to the `charts` folder.
- No window popping up.
- No manual interaction.

This matters for automation.

Step 6: Export the Excel Report

Prompt to ChatGPT

> *"Generate Python code that exports the raw sales data and weekly summaries into a formatted Excel file."*

Code

```
with pd.ExcelWriter(
    "output/reports/weekly_sales_report.xlsx",
    engine="openpyxl"
```

```
) as writer:
    df.to_excel(writer, sheet_name="Raw Data", index=False)
    weekly_summary.to_excel(writer, sheet_name="Summary", index=False)
```

At this point, the Excel report alone could be sent to the stakeholders.

Step 7: Generate the PDF Report

This is the polished version.

Prompt to ChatGPT

> *"Write Python code using ReportLab to generate a PDF report with a title, summary paragraph, a table, and an embedded chart."*

Code

```
from reportlab.platypus import SimpleDocTemplate, Paragraph, Table, Image
from reportlab.lib.styles import getSampleStyleSheet

doc = SimpleDocTemplate("output/reports/weekly_sales_report.pdf")
styles = getSampleStyleSheet()
elements = []

elements.append(Paragraph("Weekly Sales Report", styles["Title"]))
elements.append(
    Paragraph(
        "This report summarizes weekly revenue performance by region.",
        styles["Normal"]
    )
)

table_data = [weekly_summary.columns.tolist()] + weekly_summary.values.
tolist()
elements.append(Table(table_data))

elements.append(Image("output/charts/revenue_by_region.png", width=400,
height=300))

doc.build(elements)
```

What You Should See:

- A clean PDF with:
    - Title
    - Explanation
    - Table
    - Chart

Step 8: Turn It into a Pipeline

Wrap logic into functions:

```
def load_data():
    return pd.read_csv("data/sales_data.csv", parse_dates=["date"])

def clean_data(df):
    df["revenue"] = pd.to_numeric(df["revenue"], errors="coerce")
    return df.dropna(subset=["revenue"])
```

This is what separates scripts from systems.

Step 9: Final Reality Check

Before calling this "done":

- Change the data file
- Re-run the script
- Confirm that reports regenerate correctly

Automation is proven through repetition.

Conclusion

Automating data reports is not about removing yourself from the process; it is about removing friction. In this chapter, you learned how to turn a repetitive, error-prone task into a reliable system that works quietly in the background. By pairing Python with thoughtful prompts, you moved from raw data to finished reports without manual copying, formatting, or last-minute stress.

More importantly, you learned how to *design* reporting workflows, not just write scripts. You saw how data flows through cleaning, summarization, visualization, and export, and how each step builds on the one before it. With ChatGPT, you focus on decisions and structure while letting the heavy lifting happen faster and more consistently.

This skill is one of the most valuable abilities in modern technical roles. Reports change. Data sources change. Deadlines do not. Now, you have a system that adapts.

In the next chapter, we shift from offline outputs to interactive systems as we explore building an AI-Powered Web Application, where your logic becomes something that users can interact with in real time.

Points to Remember

- Automated reports save time only when the entire workflow is repeatable and structured.

- Data cleaning is not optional—it defines the accuracy of every result that follows.
- Summaries should focus on decisions, and not just numbers.
- Visualizations must be generated programmatically to support true automation.
- Export formats such as Excel and PDF serve different audiences, and should coexist.
- ChatGPT works best when prompts clearly state goals, constraints, and output format.
- A good reporting pipeline can be reused across projects with minimal changes.

Key Terms

- **Data Ingestion**: The process of loading raw data from files, databases, or APIs.
- **Data Cleaning**: Preparing data by fixing formats, handling missing values, and validating types.
- **Pandas**: A Python library for data manipulation and analysis.
- **Data Visualization**: Representing data graphically to support understanding and decisions.
- **Report Pipeline**: A sequence of automated steps that produce consistent reporting outputs.
- **ReportLab**: A Python library for programmatically generating PDF documents.
- **Openpyxl**: A Python library for reading and writing Excel files.

CHAPTER 9
Building an AI-Powered Web Application

Introduction

There is a line most developers cross at some point.

On one side of that line, you write scripts. Useful scripts. Scripts that solve real problems, but mostly for you. On the other side, you build applications that other people can touch, click, refresh, and rely on. That crossing is less about complexity and more about mindset.

This chapter is about that shift.

We are moving from "*I wrote a Python script that works*" to "*I built a web application someone else can use.*" And we are doing it with AI.

Before we go any further, let us be clear about language.

An AI-driven web app is not an app where AI magically does everything. It is an app where AI helps at specific, intentional points in the development process.

You still make decisions. The difference is that you are no longer doing it alone or guessing your way forward.

Python is often introduced through scripts, notebooks, and command-line tools. That is a good start. But most real-world impact happens when your logic lives behind a button, a form, or an API endpoint.

Web apps give you:

- **Reach:** Your code runs for anyone with a browser.
- **Persistence**: Data can be stored, updated, and reused.
- **Interactivity**: Users do not read outputs; they interact with them.
- **Credibility**: Shipping an app changes how others see your skills.

This chapter shows how to take the Python you already know, and wrap it in a structure that turns it into a usable product.

Structure

In this chapter, we will cover the following topics:

- Using AI to Scaffold Python Backend Code
- Building REST APIs with Flask
- Connecting the Python Backend to a Simple Frontend (HTML/JS)
- Error Handling and Testing with AI-Assisted Debugging

Using AI to Scaffold Python Backend Code

Most people get stuck before they even write their first line of backend logic.

Most questions revolve around:

- Which file do I create first?
- Where do routes live?
- How do I organize logic so that it does not become messy in two weeks?
- What is "too much structure" for a small app?

This is where AI earns its place in the workflow.

In this section, we will use ChatGPT to scaffold a Python backend in a way that:

- You understand every file it creates.
- You can run immediately.
- You can grow without rewrites.
- You can explain to someone else.

We will use **Flask** for clarity and simplicity. The same ideas apply to FastAPI, but Flask keeps the learning curve gentle and visible.

Step 1: Decide What We are Building

Before touching Python, we need a clear, narrow goal.

For this chapter, our backend will:

- Expose a simple API endpoint
- Accept text input from a user

- Return a processed response (later powered by AI)

That is it. No accounts. No databases.

This is important because AI works best when your request is specific.

Here is an example of a prompt you can give ChatGPT before writing any code:

> "*I want to build a small Python web backend using Flask.*
>
> *It should expose a single API endpoint that accepts text input via a POST request and returns a JSON response.*
>
> *Please scaffold a simple, beginner-friendly project structure and explain what each file does.*"

This prompt does three things:

1. Sets the framework (Flask)
2. Defines scope (single endpoint)
3. Asks for explanation, not just the code

That last part matters more than most people realize.

Step 2: Reviewing the Generated Structure

When you run a prompt like that, ChatGPT will usually return something like:

```
project/
├── app.py
├── requirements.txt
└── README.md
```

Or sometimes:

```
project/
├── app/
│   ├── __init__.py
│   ├── routes.py
│   └── services.py
├── run.py
└── requirements.txt
```

Both are valid. The difference is scale.

For learning purposes, we will start with the simpler version:

```
ai_web_app/
├── app.py
├── requirements.txt
```

You can always refactor later, once the concepts are clear.

Step 3: Installing What You Need

Open your terminal in the project folder, and install Flask:

```
pip install flask
```

```
Then, freeze dependencies:
pip freeze > requirements.txt
```

```
Your requirements.txt will now contain something like:
Flask==3.x.x
```

The exact version may differ. That is fine, use the most recent stable version available.

Step 4: Writing the Initial Backend Endpoint

Now, open `app.py`.

Instead of guessing, ask ChatGPT for a clean starting point:

> *"Write a minimal Flask app with one POST endpoint* `/api/process` *that accepts JSON input and returns a JSON response. Keep it beginner-friendly."*

A typical response looks like this:

```
from flask import Flask, request, jsonify

app = Flask(__name__)

@app.route("/api/process", methods=["POST"])
def process_text():
    data = request.get_json()
    user_text = data.get("text", "")

    return jsonify({
        "original_text": user_text,
        "message": "Text received successfully"
    })

if __name__ == "__main__":
    app.run(debug=True)
```

Before running it, slow down and read it line by line.

- **`Flask`** creates the application.
- The **`request`** gives access to incoming data.
- **`jsonify`** ensures clean JSON responses.

This line:

```
@app.route("/api/process", methods=["POST"])
```

Are you saying:

> *"I am listening here, and only for this type of request."*

At this point, we have built a standard API.

Now, we make it AI-powered.

Step 5: Integrating the AI Logic

This is the missing piece in many tutorials, and the most important one.

Install the AI Client Library

We will use the OpenAI client as an example. Install it:

```
pip install openai
```

Freeze dependencies again:

```
pip freeze > requirements.txt
```

Handling API Keys Safely

- Never hardcode API keys in your source code.
- Instead, store them as environment variables.

On macOS or Linux:

```
export OPENAI_API_KEY="your_api_key_here"
```

On Windows (PowerShell):

```
setx OPENAI_API_KEY "your_api_key_here"
```

This keeps secrets out of your codebase and version control.

Modifying the Endpoint to Call the AI

Now, we update **`process_text`** to send the user's input to the AI model, and return its response.

```
from flask import Flask, request, jsonify
import os
from openai import OpenAI

app = Flask(__name__)

client = OpenAI(api_key=os.getenv("OPENAI_API_KEY"))

@app.route("/api/process", methods=["POST"])
def process_text():
    data = request.get_json()
    user_text = data.get("text", "")
```

```
    if not user_text:
        return jsonify({"error": "No text provided"}), 400

    response = client.chat.completions.create(
        model="gpt-4o-mini",
        messages=[
            {"role": "system", "content": "You are a helpful assistant."},
            {"role": "user", "content": user_text}
        ]
    )

    ai_reply = response.choices[0].message.content

    return jsonify({
        "input": user_text,
        "ai_response": ai_reply
    })

if __name__ == "__main__":
    app.run(debug=True)
```

Now, the endpoint does not just *receive* text, it *thinks* about it.

This is the moment your app becomes genuinely AI-powered.

Step 6: Running the Backend

In your terminal:

```
python app.py
```

You should see:

```
Running on http://127.0.0.1:5000
```

Your AI backend is now live.

Step 7: Testing the AI-Powered API

Using **`curl`**:

```
curl -X POST http://127.0.0.1:5000/api/process \
-H "Content-Type: application/json" \
-d '{"text": "Explain AI in simple terms"}'
```

Example Response:

```
{
  "input": "Explain AI in simple terms",
```

```
  "ai_response": "Artificial intelligence is when computers are designed
to think and learn in ways similar to humans..."
}
```

That response means:

- Your backend works.
- Your endpoint works.
- Your structure is sound.

Building REST APIs with Flask

At this point, you already have something many beginners do not: A backend that *runs*, responds, and makes sense.

Now, we move from "a single working endpoint" to something more intentional, a REST API.

That phrase sounds heavier than it needs to be. In practice, a REST API is simply a clean agreement between your backend, and anything that talks to it: A browser, a mobile app, another service, or even your future self.

Thus, Flask does not force structure on you. That is both its strength and its danger. In this section, we will learn how to design APIs that stay readable as they grow, while using ChatGPT as a guide.

What "REST" Means

A REST API is built around a few simple ideas:

- Each endpoint represents a **resource.**
- You use HTTP methods to describe intent.
- Responses are predictable and structured.
- Errors are handled explicitly.

Thus, you have already used one method: `POST`.

Here are the most common ones you will use in real projects:

Method	Purpose
`GET`	Retrieve data
`POST`	Create or process data
`PUT`	Update the existing data
`DELETE`	Remove data

Table 9.1: *HTTP Methods*

You do not need all of them right away. But understanding the pattern early prevents confusion, later.

Step 1: Expanding Our API Intentionally

Let us say we want our app to do three things:

1. Accept the text input
2. Return a processed result
3. Expose a simple health check

Hence, before writing a code, this is a good moment to pause and ask ChatGPT for guidance.

A Useful Prompt at This Stage

> "*I have a simple Flask app with one POST endpoint.*
>
> *I want to expand it into a small REST API with clear routes and error handling.*
>
> *Please suggest endpoint names and responsibilities before writing any code.*"

This kind of prompt helps you think like an API designer.

A reasonable response might suggest:

- `/api/process → handles text input`
- `/api/status → confirms the app is running`

Let us implement both.

Step 2: Adding a GET Endpoint

Open **app.py**, and add this below your existing route.

```
@app.route("/api/status", methods=["GET"])
def status():
    return jsonify({
        "status": "running",
        "message": "API is up and responding"
    })
```

That is it.

Run the app again if it is not running:

```
python app.py
```

Visit this in your browser:

```
http://127.0.0.1:5000/api/status
```

You should see:

```
{
  "status": "running",
  "message": "API is up and responding"
}
```

This might feel trivial, but this endpoint becomes incredibly useful later, especially for monitoring, deployment checks, and debugging.

Step 3: Making POST Endpoints More Robust

Let us revisit our **`/api/process`** `route.`

Right now, it assumes a valid JSON input. That is optimistic. Real users break things.

Here is how to improve it, with the help from ChatGPT.

Prompting for Better Error Handling

> "*Improve this Flask* POST *endpoint, so it gracefully handles missing* JSON, *missing fields, and returns meaningful error responses.*"

A refined version might look like this:

```
@app.route("/api/process", methods=["POST"])
def process_text():
    if not request.is_json:
        return jsonify({"error": "Request must be JSON"}), 400

    data = request.get_json()
    text = data.get("text")

    if not text:
        return jsonify({"error": "Missing 'text' field"}), 400

    return jsonify({
        "original_text": text,
        "length": len(text),
        "message": "Text processed successfully"
    })
```

Now, your API:

- Validates input
- Communicates clearly
- Fails predictably

This is the difference between a demo and something usable.

Step 4: Testing Error Cases

Try sending bad requests intentionally.

Example: Missing JSON

```
curl -X POST http://127.0.0.1:5000/api/process
```

Response:

```
{
  "error": "Request must be JSON"
}
```

Example: Missing Field

```
curl -X POST http://127.0.0.1:5000/api/process \
-H "Content-Type: application/json" \
-d '{}'
```

Response:

```
{
  "error": "Missing 'text' field"
}
```

Testing broken cases teaches you more than the successful ones.

Step 5: Keeping Routes Readable as They Grow

As APIs grow, clutter becomes the real enemy.

Even in small apps, you should:

- Keep routes short
- Use clear names
- Avoid doing too much inside one function

If you notice a route growing long, that is a signal.

This is where ChatGPT can help refactor.

Example Prompt

> *"Refactor this Flask route to separate validation logic from processing logic, without adding unnecessary complexity."*

Use it to learn patterns.

Step 6: Why Flask Works Well for Learning APIs

Flask does not hide anything.

You see:

- How requests arrive.
- How responses are formed.
- Where logic lives.

Frameworks such as FastAPI add performance and type safety, but Flask teaches fundamentals clearly. Once you understand this, switching frameworks becomes easier.

Connecting the Python Backend to a Simple Frontend (HTML and JavaScript)

Up to this point, everything you have built lives behind the scenes. Your API works. It responds and behaves correctly.

But users do not interact with APIs directly; they interact with interfaces.

Here is how the frontend talks to the backend.

The relationship is simple:

1. The user types something into a web page.
2. JavaScript sends that data to your Flask API.
3. Flask processes the request.
4. The result is sent back as JSON.
5. JavaScript updates the page.

Once you understand this loop, everything else builds on top of it.

Step 1: Organizing Your Project Structure

Before writing the frontend code, let us put **things in the right place.**

Update your project structure like this:

```
project/
│
├── app.py
├── templates/
│   └── index.html
└── static/
    └── script.js
```

Thus, Flask expects:

- HTML files inside a `templates` folder.
- JavaScript and CSS inside a `static` folder.

This convention saves you from unnecessary configuration.

Step 2: Serving an HTML Page from Flask

Open **`app.py`** and import **`render_template`**:

```
from flask import Flask, request, jsonify, render_template
```

Add a route to serve your page:

```
@app.route("/")
def home():
    return render_template("index.html")
```

Restart the server and visit:

```
http://127.0.0.1:5000/
```

You will see a blank page for now. That is expected.

Step 3: Writing a Simple HTML Interface

Create **`templates/index.html`** and add:

```
<!DOCTYPE html>
<html lang="en">
<head>
    <meta charset="UTF-8">
    <title>AI-Powered Text Tool</title>
</head>
<body>
    <h1>Text Processor</h1>

    <textarea id="userInput" rows="6" cols="50"
        placeholder="Type or paste text here..."></textarea>
    <br><br>

    <button id="submitBtn">Process Text</button>

    <pre id="result"></pre>

    <script src="/static/script.js"></script>
</body>
</html>
```

Nothing spectacular yet. Just:

- A text area.
- A button.
- A place to display results.

This is enough for learning.

Step 4: Writing JavaScript to Call the API

Create **static/script.js** and add:

```
document.getElementById("submitBtn").addEventListener("click", async ()
=> {
    const text = document.getElementById("userInput").value;
    const resultBox = document.getElementById("result");

    if (!text) {
        resultBox.textContent = "Please enter some text.";
        return;
    }

    resultBox.textContent = "Processing...";

    try {
        const response = await fetch("/api/process", {
            method: "POST",
            headers: {
                "Content-Type": "application/json"
            },
            body: JSON.stringify({ text })
        });

        if (!response.ok) {
            throw new Error(`Server error: ${response.status}`);
        }

        const data = await response.json();
        resultBox.textContent = JSON.stringify(data, null, 2);

    } catch (error) {
        console.error("Request failed:", error);
        resultBox.textContent = `Something went wrong: ${error.
message}`;
    }
});
```

This script:

- Reads input from the page
- Sends it to your Flask API
- Displays the response

Step 5: Testing the Full Flow

a. Start your Flask app
b. Open the browser
c. Enter text
d. Click the button

You should see a response like:

```
{
  "original_text": "Hello world",
  "length": 11,
  "message": "Text processed successfully"
}
```

This moment matters.

You have connected with the:

- Browser
- JavaScript
- Backend
- Logic
- Response

That is the foundation of every modern web app.

This is a great place to use ChatGPT for clarity.

Helpful Prompt Example

> *"Explain how this JavaScript fetch call communicates with my Flask backend step by step, including what happens if the request fails."*

Use it to strengthen your understanding of the flow, not to skip it.

Common Issues (What They Teach You)

- **404 errors** → `incorrect route paths`
- **CORS errors** → `mismatch between frontend and backend domains. Occurs only when Frontend and Backend are on Different Origins`

In this chapter application, Flask serves:

- The API endpoints.
- The HTML.
- The JavaScript.

From the same origin (same domain and same port).

That means CORS errors will NOT occur in this setup.

- **JSON Errors** → `missing headers or invalid payloads`

Each one teaches something valuable about how the web works.

Error Handling and Testing with AI-Assisted Debugging

If everything worked all the time perfectly, programming would not need much thinking. But real applications often fail, and in ways you did not expect.

Thus, error handling is all about building confidence when things go wrong.

The goal is not to "avoid bugs."

The goal is to stop being afraid of them.

In scripts, errors usually stop the program, and show up clearly in your terminal.

In web apps:

- Errors can hide behind a browser refresh.
- A backend failure may show up as a blank page.
- A frontend bug may look like "nothing happens".

That is why error handling and testing are not optional, once you move beyond scripts.

Understanding from Where Errors Come

In a Flask-based web app, errors usually fall into four categories:

1. **Input Errors**: Missing or invalid data from the user.
2. **Logic Errors**: Code runs, but produces wrong results.
3. **Runtime Errors**: Exceptions during execution.
4. **Integration Errors**: Frontend and backend do not agree.

Therefore, before fixing anything, your job is to identify which category you are dealing with.

This is where ChatGPT becomes useful.

A Helpful Prompt

> *"Here is an error message from my Flask app. Help me understand what category of error this is, and what usually causes it."*

Reading Flask Error Messages Properly

Let us intentionally break something.

Modify your **`/api/process`** route:

```
@app.route("/api/process", methods=["POST"])
def process_text():
    data = request.get_json()
    text = data["text"]  # risky line

    return jsonify({
        "original_text": text,
        "length": len(text)
    })
```

Now, send an empty JSON object.

Your terminal might show something such as:

```
KeyError: 'text'
```

This is not a Flask problem.

It is Python telling you exactly what happened.

So, instead of rushing to fix it, ask ChatGPT the right question.

Better Prompt

> *"This Flask route throws a KeyError when the 'text' field is missing. Explain why this happens and how to guard against it without hiding the error."*

The explanation matters more than the code.

Writing Defensive Code

A common beginner mistake is swallowing errors silently.

Instead, aim for:

- Clear validation.
- Explicit error messages.
- Meaningful HTTP status codes.

Here is a balanced version:

```
@app.route("/api/process", methods=["POST"])
def process_text():
    if not request.is_json:
        return jsonify({"error": "Expected JSON input"}), 400

    data = request.get_json()
    if "text" not in data:
        return jsonify({"error": "Missing 'text' field"}), 400

    text = data["text"]

    return jsonify({
        "original_text": text,
        "length": len(text)
    })
```

This protects your app and tells users what went wrong.

Debugging Frontend Errors with Intention

Now, let us break the frontend.

Change your JavaScript fetch call to this:

```
fetch("/api/process", {  // typo here
    method: "POST",
    headers: {
        "Content-Type": "application/json"
    },
    body: JSON.stringify({ text })
});
```

Click the button > Nothing happens.

Open the browser's developer console. You will likely see:

```
404 (NOT FOUND)
```

This is not a JavaScript bug.

It is a routing mismatch.

Instead of asking ChatGPT to "fix my code," ask:

> "*My frontend fetch request returns a 404 error.*
>
> *What should I check first in a Flask + JavaScript setup?*"

Good debugging starts with good questions.

Using ChatGPT to Debug, Not Guess

When using ChatGPT for debugging, always provide the context.

Bad prompt:

> *"My Flask app is not working."*

Better prompt:

> *"This Flask route works when tested with curl, but fails when called from JavaScript. Here is the route, the fetch call, and the error message."*

Thus, you are training yourself to think clearly.

Basic Testing without Extra Tools

You do not need a full testing framework yet.

Simple testing habits go a long way:

- Test endpoints with curl or Postman
- Refresh the browser after backend changes
- Print intermediate values during development
- Break things on purpose

Ask ChatGPT questions like:

```
"What edge cases should I test for this endpoint?"
```

That is how testing becomes a habit.

Knowing When Not to Trust AI Suggestions

AI can suggest fixes that:

- Silence errors without solving them
- Add unnecessary complexity
- Mask deeper logic issues

Always ask yourself:

- Do I understand why this fix works?
- Does it improve clarity?
- Would I write this myself next time?

If the answer is no, slow down.

Conclusion

This chapter marked a turning point. Until now, most of your work has lived in scripts, useful but mostly invisible. Here, you crossed into building something people can actually *use*. You designed a backend, connected it to a frontend, handled errors thoughtfully, and learned how AI fits into the process without taking control away from you.

More importantly, you learned a transferable skill: how to grow a Python idea into a user-facing application. The tools will change over time, Flask today, something else tomorrow, but the thinking you practiced here will remain relevant. You now understand how requests flow, how logic is exposed safely, and how AI can support design, debugging, and iteration without replacing judgment.

In the next chapter, we shift our focus again, this time toward best practices and optimization, where you will learn how to make your AI-assisted code faster, cleaner, more reliable, and easier to maintain as projects grow.

Hands-on Project: Build a Mini AI-Powered Web Application

(No Solution Provided: Follow the steps and use prompts to guide yourself)

Your goal is to build a small, working AI-powered web app. Choose any one of the following:

- A text summarizer
- A chatbot
- A sentiment analyzer

You will use Flask, HTML/JavaScript, and ChatGPT prompts to guide your implementation.

Define the Purpose

Prompt Yourself (and ChatGPT):

"Help me clearly define the goal of a small AI-powered web app.

What input will the user provide, and what output should they see?"

Write this down before touching the code.

Scaffold the Backend

Ask ChatGPT:

> *"Create a simple Flask app structure for a web API that accepts user input and returns processed text."*

Implement:

- One GET route (status or homepage).
- One POST route for processing input/

Design the API Contract

Before coding logic, ask:

> *"What should my request and response JSON look like for this app?"*

Decide:

- Required fields
- Error responses
- Success responses

Build the Frontend

Create:

- A text input area.
- A submit button.
- A result display section.

Prompt ChatGPT:

> *"Write a minimal HTML + JavaScript frontend that sends user input to a Flask POST endpoint and displays the response."*

Make sure it works end-to-end.

Integrate AI Logic

Now, bring in AI processing.

Prompt carefully:

> *"Given this Flask route, show how I can integrate an AI API call safely and return the processed result."*

Focus on:

- Input validation
- Clear outputs
- Graceful error handling

Handle Errors and Edge Cases

Break your app on purpose:

- Empty input
- Invalid JSON
- Network failure

Ask ChatGPT:

"What edge cases should I test for in this application, and how should I handle them?"

Implement fixes you understand.

Improve Structure

Finally, ask:

"How can I refactor this Flask app to improve readability and separation of concerns without overengineering?"

Clean up your code.

If a real user can interact with your app without confusion, you are done.

Key Terms

- **REST API:** A structured way for different systems (such as a browser and a server) to communicate using predictable URLs and request types.
- **Endpoint:** A specific URL in a web application that performs one action, such as processing input or returning data.
- **HTTP Methods:** Standard actions (GET, POST, and so on) that describe what a request intends to do, not how it does it.
- **Request-Response Cycle:** The full journey of data: A request sent by the user, processed by the server, and returned as a response.
- **Frontend-Backend Integration:** The connection between what users see (HTML/JavaScript) and the logic that runs behind the scenes (Python).

- **Error Handling:** The practice of anticipating failure, and responding with clear, meaningful messages, instead of crashes or silence.

Points to Remember

- **Web Applications are Conversations, Not Scripts**

  Every action involves input, processing, and feedback; understanding this flow makes debugging easier.

- **Good APIs are Designed before They are Coded**

  Thinking about routes, inputs, and outputs early prevents confusion as the project grows.

- **Error Messages are Part of Your Interface**

  A clear error helps both users and future developers understand what went wrong.

- **AI is Most Useful When You Already Have Context**

  The better your prompt and explanation, the more accurate and helpful the output becomes.

- **Simplicity Beats Cleverness in Backend Design**

  Straightforward code is easier to test, fix, and extend than tightly packed logic.

- **If You can Explain Your App out Loud, You Understand It**

  Clarity in explanation usually reflects clarity in structure and thinking.

CHAPTER 10
Best Practices and Optimization

Introduction

Now comes the part many developers skip.

This final chapter is about **longevity**. Code that survives changing requirements, new teammates, growing data, and future versions of Python. It is about learning to look at your own work with a slightly more critical eye, not to find fault, but to improve clarity, reliability, and performance.

We will zoom out a bit. Software does not live in isolation. It is read, modified, deployed, and maintained by people, often long after the original author has moved on. This chapter ties everything together by showing how to use AI to support collaboration, documentation, and forward-looking decisions, so that your work does not just solve today's problem, but remains useful tomorrow.

Structure

In this chapter, we will cover the following topics:

- Writing Clean, Readable Python Code (PEP 8 and AI-assisted reviews)
- Testing Strategies: Unit Tests with Pytest and AI-Assisted Test Case Generation
- Version Control and Collaboration with GitHub
- Future Directions

Writing Clean, Readable Python Code

There is a moment every developer experiences, usually a few months into a project, when they open a file they once wrote and think:

"Why did I do it like this?"

Clean, readable code is not about showing how clever you are. It is about leaving behind something that still makes sense when time has passed, context has faded, and someone else sometimes in future or you have to work with it.

Clean code in Python has three defining qualities:

- It is easy to read.
- It is easy to reason.
- It is easy to change.

Notice what is missing from that list: clever tricks, compressed one-liners, or "advanced" patterns used too early. Python's strength has always been clarity, and good Python code leans into that strength, instead of fighting it.

The fastest way to make code unreadable is poor naming.

Compare these two examples:

```
def calc(x, y):
    return x * y * 0.1
```

Versus:

```
def calculate_discount(price, discount_rate):
    return price * discount_rate
```

Both work. Only one explains itself.

Before changing the logic, ask ChatGPT questions like:

> *"Given this function and its usage, suggest clearer variable and function names."*

Small Functions Beat Smart Functions

If a function does more than one thing, it is doing too much.

Instead of writing one long function that:

- Reads data
- Processes it
- Formats output
- Writes to disk

Break it into steps that can be named and understood independently.

Example:

```
def load_sales_data(path):
    ...

def calculate_totals(data):
    ...

def generate_report(totals):
    ...
```

Each function becomes easier to test, reuse, and explain.

A useful prompt here is:

> *"Help me split this function into smaller, single-purpose functions without changing behavior."*

Readable code relies more on structure than comments.

Good structure uses:

- Consistent indentation
- Logical spacing
- Grouped related operations
- Clear ordering of imports, constants, functions, and execution

Thus, instead of explaining what code does, aim for code that makes explanations unnecessary.

ChatGPT can help review structure with prompts like:

> *"Review this Python file for readability and structural clarity. Suggest improvements without adding complexity."*

PEP 8: A Shared Language, not a Rulebook

PEP 8 is not about style policing. It is about shared expectations.

Following it means:

- Anyone familiar with Python can read your code faster.
- Tools behave more predictably.
- Teams argue less about formatting.

That said, understanding *why* a rule exists matters more than memorizing it.

For example:

- Line length limits improve scanning.

- Consistent naming reduces mental load.
- Spacing makes logic easier to follow.

Instead of asking AI to "fix PEP 8 issues," ask:

> *"Explain which PEP 8 suggestions improve readability here and which ones are optional."*

Using AI as a Code Reviewer

The most effective way to use AI at this stage is as a reviewer.

After writing code yourself, try:

> *"Review this code as if you were a teammate.*
> *Focus on clarity, naming, and maintainability."*

Then decide what to keep and what to ignore.

You are still responsible for the final call.

A clean code often emerges through refactoring, not first drafts.

Refactoring means:

- Changing structure without changing behavior.
- Improving names, flow, and organization.
- Making future changes safer.

Before refactoring, make sure that you understand the code. During refactoring, make small changes. After refactoring, test again.

AI can help you move carefully by explaining *why* a refactor helps, not just showing *how*.

Testing Strategies: Unit Tests with Pytest and AI-Assisted Test Case Generation

Testing is how you make sure your code works now, and keeps working as it grows. For beginners, testing might feel optional but in real-world projects, it is non-negotiable. This section focuses on simple, practical testing using pytest, plus how to use AI to think like a tester.

Why Testing Matters

Testing helps you:

- Catch bugs before users do.

- Refactor code without fear.
- Understand your own logic better.
- Build confidence in your work.

Unit Testing

Unit testing means testing small, isolated pieces of code (usually functions).

If you write a function that adds two numbers:

A unit test checks: Does this function always return the correct result for different inputs?

You are testing behavior, not the whole app.

Pytest

`pytest` is one of the most popular Python testing tools because it is:

- Simple to read and write.
- Powerful without being complex.
- Widely used in real companies.

So, you do not need classes or complicated setup to get started.

Basic Pytest Structure (Conceptual)

A typical test follows this pattern:

1. **Arrange** - prepare inputs
2. **Act** – call the function
3. **Assert** – check the result

In plain language:

"When I give this input, I expect this output."

Example ideas of what you test:

- Correct results
- Wrong inputs
- Edge cases (empty values, zero, negative numbers)

Writing Your First Meaningful Tests

Good tests:

- Are small and focused

- Test one thing at a time
- Have clear names that explain *what* is being tested

Bad tests:

- Try to test everything at once
- Depend on other tests
- Are hard to understand

If a test fails, you should immediately know why.

Edge Cases: Where Bugs Usually Hide

Beginners often test only "`happy paths`", inputs that obviously work.

Real bugs show up when:

- Input is empty.
- Input is unexpected.
- Values are very large or very small.
- Types are wrong (string instead of number).

Testing edge cases is what separates beginners from experts.

Using AI to Generate Better Test Cases

AI is extremely useful for thinking like a tester.

Instead of asking AI to "write tests for me", use prompts that guide reasoning.

Example prompt patterns:

- "*List edge cases for this function.*"
- "*What inputs could break this logic?*"
- "*Generate test scenarios for real-world usage.*"
- "*What assumptions does this function make?*"

You stay in control.

AI-assisted Debugging When Tests Fail

When a test fails:

1. Read the error message carefully.
2. Identify what failed, not just that it failed.

3. Ask AI questions like:
   - *"Why would this assertion fail?"*
   - *"What could cause this function to return None?"*
   - *Explain this error message in simple terms."*

This helps you to learn faster, not just fix bugs blindly.

When to Write Tests in a Project

Good habits:

- Write tests as soon as a function works.
- Add tests when fixing a bug.
- Test critical logic first (auth, payments, calculations, and so on).

Version Control and Collaboration with GitHub

Writing clean codes is only a part of being a professional developer. Equally important is how that code is tracked, shared, reviewed, and improved over time. This is where version control and GitHub, in particular, becomes essential.

If Python is the language you write in, Git is the memory of your project.

Without version control, development becomes fragile:

- You overwrite working code, while experimenting.
- You cannot easily return to an earlier version.
- Collaboration turns into file-sharing chaos.
- Bugs become difficult to trace back to their origin.

Hence, Git solves these problems by recording every meaningful change to your codebase. Each change is intentional, reversible, and documented.

You do not need to master every Git command to be effective. At a minimum, understand these ideas:

- **Repository (repo):** A tracked project folder.
- **Commit:** A snapshot of changes with a message explaining *why*.
- **Branch:** A parallel version of the code for safe experimentation.
- **Remote:** A hosted copy of your repository (for example, GitHub)

Think of Git as a timeline of decisions.

A simple, professional Git workflow.

A clean workflow reinforces a clean code.

Initialize a repository

```
git init
```

1. **Track your files**

   ```
   git add .
   ```

2. **Commit with intention**

   ```
   git commit -m "Add data validation for user input"
   ```

3. Good commit messages explain why the change exists, not just what changed.

Using GitHub as a Development Partner:

GitHub is more than a backup service. It is a collaboration and learning platform.

- **Pull Requests (PRs):** Propose changes and review the code before merging.
- **Issues:** Track bugs, ideas, and improvements.
- **Commit history:** Understand how a project evolved.

Even as a solo developer, using pull requests helps you slow down and review your own work critically.

Using AI to improve your Git practices:

AI fits naturally into version control workflows when used deliberately.

Examples of helpful prompts:

- `"Review this commit diff and suggest improvements before I push it."`
- `"Help me write a clear commit message for these changes."`
- `"Does this pull request introduce any hidden risks?"`
- `"Suggest a branching strategy for a small Python web app."`

Version Control as a Learning Tool

One underrated benefit of Git is reflection.

By reviewing old commits, you can:

- See how your thinking has improved.
- Understand when bugs were introduced.
- Learn from past design decisions.

Many experienced developers credit version control with accelerating their growth not because of the tool itself, but because it forces intentional development.

Conclusion

This chapter marked a shift from *writing code that works* to *writing code that lasts*. You learned that professionalism in software development is not just about features, but about clarity, structure, safety, and collaboration.

By exploring clean code principles, testing strategies, and performance awareness, you saw how AI can act as a reviewer, mentor, and productivity partner.

Thus, as you move forward, remember that good developers solve problems, but *great developers solve them in a way that others can understand, trust, and extend.* With Python and AI as your tools, you now have everything you need to grow into that role.

Future Directions

So, you have reached to the end of this chapter, but not the end of the journey. What you have learned here is a foundation, not a finish line. The real value comes from how you build on it deliberately.

Deepen Your Python Fundamentals

Before chasing advanced tools, make sure your core is strong.

Focus on:

- Writing reusable functions and modules.
- Working confidently with lists, dictionaries, and classes.
- Reading other people's Python codes, and understanding them.

A *strong foundation will make every future topic easier.*

Build More Small, Real Projects

Progress in software comes from doing, not watching tutorials.

Good next project ideas:

- A task manager (CLI or web-based).
- A simple API that stores and retrieves data.
- A basic dashboard that displays user input.
- A mini automation tool that solves a personal problem.

Small projects teach you more than big plans that never ship.

Go Deeper into Testing and Debugging

Thus, you have seen how testing protects your code. Now expand that habit.

Next steps:

- Write tests before writing logic (test-first thinking).
- Learn how to test APIs and user input.
- Practice debugging using error messages, logs, and tests.

This is where you start thinking like a professional engineer.

Learn Basic Backend Architecture

As projects grow, structure matters.

Explore:

- How backend files are organized.
- How APIs communicate with frontends.
- How to separate logic, data, and the presentation.
- How environment variables and configuration work.

Use AI as a Long-term Learning Partner

AI will stay with you throughout your career, and hence, how you use it matters.

Use AI to:

- Explain unfamiliar errors.
- Suggest edge cases and improvements.
- Review your code for clarity.
- Help you plan projects step-by-step.

Avoid using AI to skip learning. Use it to accelerate understanding.

Start Sharing What You Learn

Teaching is one of the fastest ways to grow.

You can:

- Write short posts about what you learned.
- Document your projects clearly.
- Explain concepts in simple language to others.
- Share mistakes and lessons, not just wins.

This builds confidence and real-world credibility.

Key Terms

- **Clean Code:** Code that is easy to read, understand, and maintain by both the original author and others over time.
- **PEP 8:** The official Python style guide that defines best practices for formatting, naming, and structuring Python code.
- **Unit Testing:** A testing approach where individual functions or components are tested in isolation to ensure correctness.
- **Pytest:** A popular Python testing framework that makes writing and running tests simple and expressive.
- **Refactoring:** The process of improving the structure and readability of a code without changing its behavior.

Points to Remember

- **Readable code is more valuable than clever code.**

  The code is read far more often than it is written, so clarity should always come first.
- **Testing is a safety net, not a burden.**

  Tests help you make changes confidently, and catch bugs before they reach the users.
- **AI works best as a reviewer and a coach.**

  Use AI to improve structure, suggest tests, and explain errors — not to avoid thinking.
- **Performance awareness grows with experience.**

  Start by writing a clear code first, then optimize only when necessary, and with evidence.
- **Growth comes from consistent practice, not perfection.**

  Small projects, regular reviews, and continuous learning will take you further than any single tool or framework.

Index

B

C